"**WOW!** One of the hardest-hitting books I've ever laid eyes on! <u>STOP IT!</u> puts Consumers back in control of their lives! A *must* read for anyone on the ropes!"
- Barry Young, KFYI Radio-Phoenix

"**OFF THE METER!!!**"
- Richard Walker, KRLD Radio-Dallas

"**FINALLY!** A book designed for Consumers to put to work *immediately*, <u>STOP IT!</u> turns the tables on the Debt Collectors across the country!"
- Sean Casey, WCBM Radio-Baltimore

"**DOVER & HIBBS <u>DELIVER!</u>** Strap on the hand grenades and get ready for war with <u>STOP IT!</u>"
- Bob Ray Sanders, KLIF Radio-Dallas

STOP IT!

A Consumer's Guide To
Effectively Stopping
Collection Agency Harassment

by Bud Hibbs

edited by
Benjamin Dover
&
Andy Grieser

Published by
Equitable Media Services
Fort Worth, Texas

The following company names appear in this book and are registered trademarks of their respective companies: Kwik Kopy, AlphaGraphics, Radio Shack, TRW, TransUnion, Equifax Credit Information Services.

U.S. Government publications, Federal Trade Commission, Facts for Consumers, September, 1991, Washington, D.C.
U.S. Government publications, Federal Trade Commission, Public Law 95-109, Consumer Credit Protection Act, Amendments, Washington, D.C.

Tom & Marilyn Ross, The Complete Guide to Self-Publishing, Second Edition © 1989, reprinted by permission of Writer's Digest Books, Cincinnati, Ohio.

For more information, contact: David Flowers/Media Coordinator, Equitable Media Services, Post Office Box 9822, Fort Worth, Texas 76147-2822.

Library of Congress Cataloging In Publication Data
Library of Congress Catalog Card Number: 91-77795
Hibbs, Bud
  STOP IT! A Consumer's Guide to
  Effectively Stopping Collection Agency Harassment
  1. Consumer Law
  2. Federal Law
ISBN 1-880925-00-1

i

DEDICATION

This book is dedicated to all of the people in America who have had to endure hardship as a direct result of the unethical, immoral, selfish, petty, unprincipled and generally self-serving conduct of **THE COLLECTION AGENCY.**

Thank you Susan, Lance & Sheen.

"Tough times don't last. Tough people *do*."
                                             - Old Texas proverb

PREFACE

WARNING!
THIS BOOK IS LETHAL!

By using this book, you could contribute to the failure of Collection Agencies throughout the country.

The knowledge you are about to harness can and will directly affect the livelihoods of collection agency employees, their owners and legal representatives.

The knowledge contained within the covers of this book will help you end the relentless pursuit of The Collection Agency... and (best of all) will keep them from earning a living off of your difficult situation. Most importantly, you will be able to LEGALLY PROHIBIT THE COLLECTION AGENCY AND THEIR REPRESENTATIVES FROM EVER CONTACTING YOU AGAIN.

IMPORTANT NOTICE: Read this book thoroughly before taking action against any and all creditors/Collection Agencies. You need the complete knowledge, perspective and strategy provided between the two covers of this book.

If you fail to read all chapters and begin your offensive against those who are currently making your life hell, *you are at risk of taking the wrong or inappropriate action for your particular situation.*

You will be encouraged and excited as you progress through this book. Don't make the mistake of going off *"half-cocked."*

Read the book twice before you commence your counter-attack.

Knowledge is <u>power</u>. Use it effectively!

DISCLAIMER

I am not an attorney and do not give legal advice. This book does not in any way attempt to dispense legal advice. It is solely intended to share my proven methods of effectively invoking provisions of the Fair Debt Collection Practices Act to end all communication with collection agencies or their legal representatives.

- Bud Hibbs
April 1992

TABLE OF CONTENTS

APPENDIX J
Sample Letter Format Utilized To

Chapter I

THE COLLECTION AGENCY

*"There's one way to find out if a man is honest...ask him.
If he says Yes, you know he is a crook."*
                                        - Groucho Marx

Collection Agency...just the name is enough to turn most peoples' stomachs.

Don't feel bad; you are not alone.

The majority of people who have dealt with Collection Agencies will be the first to tell you their experiences were anything but pleasant.

Collection Agencies are out to make a buck...a real fast buck at your expense. I really shouldn't let my personal feelings surface here, but in my opinion, Collection Agents should rank well below lawyers, used car salesmen and home aluminum siding salesmen on Life's Bottom Ten Trustworthy Professions.

Please understand that there are some very good, credible Collection Agencies/Agents throughout the country.

1

STOP IT!

Collection Agencies are a *"necessary evil"*...They are needed to assist all types of companies in receiving payment for goods or services they have provided the consumer in good faith.

It is not what they do here that we are going to discuss, but *how* they do it.

STOP IT! will explain how Collection Agencies work and what they can or cannot legally say or do in order to achieve results for their clients.

STOP IT! will give you an insight into the methods utilized by Collection Agencies...methods which include, but are not limited to, threats, intimidation, coercion, blackmail and fear. Sounds like tactics reserved for convicted felons, doesn't it?

Collection Agencies have been around for a long time. Normally, their representatives will call you and politely try to work things out when your debt has become delinquent with an original creditor. By the time your account has been assigned to a Collection Agency, it has usually been "written off" by the original creditor. When an account has been "written off," this means it has been charged off of their Accounts Receivables to an account on their income statement commonly known as "Bad Debt Expense."

Once an account has been charged off to the Bad Debt Expense category, the creditor is admitting it feels its chances of recovering the debt are slim to none. Therefore, it either: **a)** sells off their bad debts to a Collection Agency at a very deep discount (i.e., 10 cents of every dollar owed on the outstanding accounts) or **b)** assigns them to a Collection Agency on a "contingency" basis. This means the Collection

2

The Collection Agency

Agency attempts to collect the debt for the original creditor and, if successful, splits the money recovered with the original creditor. The funds kept by the Collection Agency can range from 30% to 70% of the split. The balance is remitted to the original creditor, who then credits it back to their Profit & Loss Statement (commonly referred to as P&L) under the "Bad Debt Recovery" category.

The purpose of illustrating this whole scenario to you is simple: once you understand a Collection Agency's motivation, you can stop it quickly from annoying you any further. It's motivation is easy to calculate. Suppose you have an account with ACME Department Store that has been assigned to a Collection Agency. You've got a $1,000 balance that you cannot pay for whatever reason.*

ACME assigned this account to ABC Collection Agency on a 50/50 split basis. This means if ABC Collection Agency is successful at collecting the $1,000 debt in full, they will receive 50% (or $500) for their efforts. In most cases, the people who work for the Collection Agencies (known as "agents," "collection agents," "account representatives," "debt collectors," etc.) work for an hourly wage **plus** a commission or percentage of the total monies they recover.

Using the players described in the previous paragraphs, I'll attempt to illustrate a typical relationship between the debtor (John Doe), the original creditor (ACME Department Store), the Collection Agency (ABC Collection Agency) and the individual Collection Agency Agent (Tom Smith).

---

*-Reasons can include but not be limited to: lost job, family illness, divorce, result of a bad debt, etc.

3

STOP IT!

To make all illustrations throughout the remainder of this book easier to understand and follow, we will utilize the same example names throughout. All sample letters, U.S. Post Office paperwork, Cease & Desist Letters, etc., will bear the same character example names.

John Doe, the debtor, owes ACME Department Store money on his revolving charge card that he cannot repay:	$1,000
ACME assigns the debt to ABC Collection Agency on a 50/50 split basis. (In this example, we will assume the debt is fully repaid.)	$500 to ABC $500 to ACME
ABC Collection assigns the account to their top Collection Agent, Tom Smith. Tom is paid $6.00 per hour, PLUS a bonus equal to 50% of all of money he recovers.	2 hours x $6 per hour -------------- $12 plus $250 bonus

Tom Smith spends an average of five minutes on the phone with you once a week over a 6-month period. This adds up to 20 minutes a month, or 120 minutes (two hours) over a 6-month collection/repayment period. Tom Smith is guaranteed his $6 per hour, but the real money comes from the accounts he successfully collects. He clocked two hours on your account over the 6-month period...but his real money was made on the money he got John Doe to repay on his ACME Department Store account: 50% of the $500 received by ABC Collection Agency, a $250 commission, plus the $12 (hourly) wage =

$262 NET PAY.

Poor John Doe. Aside from all of the financial problems he is having to endure, he ends up paying Tom Smith, the Collection Agent, what amounts to an hourly wage of $131 to regularly harass him through the mail and over the phone, both at work and at home. In addition, ACME Department Stores and ABC Collection have destroyed John Doe's credit record with negative remarks... remarks that will stay in place for up to seven years.

The Collection Agency

Since you now have a better idea of the motivations through this chain, it's easy to understand why the Collection Agency many times reverts to tougher and tougher tactics. Frankly, their tactics cross the border and are clearly, according to federal laws, criminal.

Collection Agency activities became more and more radical through the years and were uncontrolled. Unbelievable as it may seem, Collection Agencies wrote their own rules, since there was no uniform regulatory agency on a national scale to monitor their activities.

With complaints and horror stories mounting, the United States Congress enacted Public Law 95-109, more commonly known as **THE FAIR DEBT COLLECTION PRACTICES ACT,** in 1977.

This legislation was passed to prohibit abusive practices utilized by Debt Collectors. In the chapters that follow, based on my firsthand experience, you will learn the most effective use of this law to end Collection Agency harassment.

Forever.

Chapter II

UNDERSTANDING THE LAW

*"It ain't no sin if you crack a few laws now and then,
just so long as you don't break any."*
                                                    - Mae West

When I first became interested in Public Law 95-109, I
consulted with many friends of mine who happened to be
attorneys. When asked what I, a consumer, could do to utilize
this law to my advantage, their responses were identical:
"Go to the library and do what we do...read, read and read."

So I went to the library and followed their advice. I read. I
wrote to various federal agencies in Washington and asked
them to send to me all of the information available in any area
remotely relating to debtor/creditor relationships. The more I
read and researched, the better I understood the power that you
and I, the consumer/debtor, really have.

Public Law 95-109 **(The Fair Debt Collection Practices Act)**
was obviously enacted to regulate the activities Debt Collector/
Collection Agencies utilized to recover monies owed to
creditors.

Not so obvious are the rights of the consumer/debtor. We'll
explore 10 key areas covered in this valuable piece of
legislation.

Chapter III

ACQUISITION OF INFORMATION

*"It takes a wise man to handle a lie;
a fool had better remain honest."*
- Norman Douglas

When a Collection Agency/Debt Collector (hereinafter referred to as "Collector") is attempting to locate a debtor for the purpose of collecting a debt, the law specifically states that he/she shall:

1) Not tell the party contacted (such as work supervisor, next-door neighbor, etc.) that the purpose of the call is to collect a debt.

2) Identify him/herself and say he/she is confirming or correcting information concerning the debtor and only, if specifically asked to, identify him/herself and employer.

3) Not communicate with any third party (such as work supervisor, next-door neighbor, etc.) more than once unless the Collector believes the information supplied is erroneous or incomplete.

4) Not mail anything to you, either at home or place of employment, on a postcard.

STOP IT!

5) Not use any type of envelope, mailgram, telegram or other communication to allow anyone to know the Collector is in the debt collection business (this part of the law is designed to keep the Collector from embarrassing you, the debtor/consumer).

6) Not communicate with you once you have notified the Collector that you are represented by an attorney and have properly noticed the Collector of the name/address of your attorney.

SIMPLY RESTATED: The Collectors cannot embarrass you by talking with your co-workers, neighbors, relatives, etc., about your situation. The Collectors cannot continue to call you about your debt(s) once you have given them your attorney's name (if you have one and if an attorney is actually needed).

Chapter IV

COMMUNICATION WITH YOU/OTHERS
ABOUT YOUR DEBT

"Archie doesn't know how to worry without getting upset."
- Edith Bunker of "All in the Family"

Unless you (the debtor) specifically give your permission to the Collector (or unless they have a court order), a Collector may **NOT** communicate with you in the collection of any debt:

1) Prior to 8 a.m. or after 9 p.m. (your local time).

2) If you have duly notified/supplied the Collector with the name/address of the attorney representing you.

3) At your place of employment if the Collector has reason to believe the employer prohibits you from receiving such calls.

For example, when a Collector calls you at work, ask him/her to state their name and company they work for and then say the following:

"Mr. (Ms.) Collector, my supervisor has asked me to inform you that this type of call is not allowed to be received here, where I work. If you should ever call me here again, I will

11

STOP IT!

file a complaint against you and your company with the Federal Trade Commission."

Remember, you are dealing with people who have questionable morals and equally questionable intelligence. Expect them to come back with a dumb remark...you won't be disappointed (I'll show you how to handle this later in the book).

4) And may not communicate with anyone except you, your attorney or a consumer credit reporting agency about your debt. More plainly stated, this means a Collector cannot call or threaten to call your family, friends or neighbors. If the Collector does contact anyone not authorized to be involved in your situation, **THEY ARE BREAKING THE LAW.**

If the Collector is willing to resort to these types of techniques, you should not be reluctant to **"fight fire with fire."**

Don't be shy: call and write to the Federal Trade Commission and file a complaint about the tactics employed by the Collector. Many state and local governments have rules and regulations similar to the federal laws designed to protect the debtor/consumer. You need to make sure these laws are enforced.

Don't be afraid to push back! Get tough with the Collector and let them know that you know the laws and will cause them a lot of problems if they push you again. Then follow it up. Back up your threat. The law is on your side.

5) If you duly notify a Collection Agency that they are to cease all further communication with you, they shall not communicate with you any further, except to state that they are

Communication With You/Others About Your Debt

terminating their collection effort, or to notify you that either the Debt Collector or original creditor intend to invoke specific remedies (that are normal and/or acceptable) to satisfy the debt (such as the pursuit of legal action).

PLEASE NOTE: It is absolutely imperative you give notice to either the original creditor or the Collection Agency/Debt Collector that they have assigned your account to, through the only recognized and legal method...the U.S. Postal Service.

You must send the original creditor or the Collection Agency/Debt Collector any and all notices via Certified Letter, Return Receipt Requested (complete instructions for this method are outlined later in this book).

DO NOT attempt to call either the original creditor or the Collection Agency/Debt Collector or send them any written correspondence via regular mail. They will deny ever hearing from you, since these methods are not considered as "Delivery Methods of Record."

SIMPLY RESTATED:
   (a) The Collectors cannot call you in the middle of the night or early in the morning;
   (b) Once you've told them your attorney's name, they cannot continue to hound you over the debt(s);
   (c) The Collectors cannot call you at your place of employment if they suspect it could cause problems with your employer;
   (d) The Collector is restricted by law from discussing your situation with **ANYONE** but you (the debtor), your attorney, the original creditor or a recognized credit reporting agency. **PERIOD. NO EXCEPTIONS.**

Chapter V

HARASSMENT OR ABUSE

"All cruelness springs from weakness."
- Seneca (4 B.C.-A.D. 65)

A Collector is not legally allowed to engage in any conduct that may harass, abuse or oppress you in the connection with the collection of a debt. The following conduct is considered in violation:

1) If the Collector uses or threatens to use violence or other criminal means to harm the physical person, reputation or property of the person.

2) The use of obscene or profane language or language that abuses the listener or person reading such language.

3) The publication of any list that shows consumers who allegedly refuse to pay a debt (except to a credit bureau).

4) Either threatening or actually posting the debt for sale in order to coerce repayment of the debt.

5) Causing a telephone to ring or engaging a person in telephone conversation repeatedly or continuously with intent

15

STOP IT!

to annoy, abuse or harass any person at the number called (this is the most common complaint).

SIMPLY RESTATED: The Collectors cannot threaten you in <u>*ANY*</u> way, shape or form, nor can they blackmail you into repaying the debt by threatening to sell it to a third party. Likewise, they cannot use the telephone as an instrument of harassment.

Chapter VI

FALSE OR MISLEADING REPRESENTATIONS

"Fraud and falsehood only dread examination.
Truth invites it."
- Thomas Cooper (1759-1851)

A Collector may not use any false, deceptive or misleading representation or means in connection with the collection of any debt. The following examples are common examples of violations in this area:

1) The false representation or implication that the Collector is vouched for, bonded by or affiliated with either a federal or state government agency. This shall include, but not be limited to, the use of any badge, uniform or facsimile of (this includes the collection of student loans).

2) The false representation of the nature, amount or legal status of any debt, or services rendered or compensation paid to a Debt Collector for the collection of a debt.

3) False representation that the Debt Collector is an attorney, or the communication is from an attorney. Example: "I represent the legal department of..."

4) Falsely representing that if you do not pay the debt, your action could result in your arrest or imprisonment, or that it

17

STOP IT!

could result in seizure of property, garnishment of pay or sale of property unless such action is lawful, and that the debt collector or creditor intends to take such action.

5) Other prohibited or misleading representations including, but not limited to:
   a) the consumer committed a crime;
   b) threatening to tell others about your debt;
   c) the sending of any written communication to others notifying them of your debt;
   d) deceptive means of collecting the debt;
   e) false representation that documents are legal process;
   f) stating that the Collector works for a credit bureau.

SIMPLY RESTATED: The Collectors are not allowed to lie, deceive or threaten you into repaying your debt.

Chapter VII

UNFAIR PRACTICES

"The victor will never be asked if he told the truth."
- Adolf Hitler

A Collector is restricted by law against using unfair or dishonest means to collect or attempt to collect a debt. The following are considered violations of this law:

1) The collection of any amount such as interest, fees or charges other than the principal amount, unless it is expressly authorized by the agreement creating the debt and/or permitted by law.

2) The Collector taking checks from you that are postdated more than five days, unless the Collector notifies you no more than 10 or less than three business days prior to depositing the check.

3) The solicitation by a Collector of any postdated check for the purpose of threatening or instituting criminal prosecution.

4) Depositing or threatening to deposit any postdated check prior to the date of such check.

STOP IT!

5) Causing charges to be incurred by the debtor for communications by concealing the true purpose of the communication. Example: A Collector calling you collect.

6) Taking or threatening to take any nonjudicial action to effect dispossession or disablement of property if:
   a) there is no present right to property;
   b) there is no intent to take possession;
   c) the property is exempt from such action.

7) Communicating with you by postcard.

8) Using any language or symbol other than the Debt Collector's address on any envelope when communicating with a consumer by mail or by telegram. The Collector may use its business name if it does not indicate the business is Debt Collection.

SIMPLY RESTATED: Another chapter of the law designed to further restrict the Collector's ability to lie, deceive, coerce or embarrass you into repaying the outstanding debt.

Chapter VIII

VALIDATION OF DEBTS

"When I was young I thought that money was the most important thing in life; now that I am old, I know it is."
- Oscar Wilde (1854-1900)

Within five days after the initial communication with a consumer/debtor in connection with the collection of a debt, a Collector shall, unless the following information is contained in the initial communication or the consumer/debtor has paid the debt, send the consumer/debtor a written notice containing:

1) The amount of the debt;

2) The name of the creditor to whom the debt is owed;

3) A statement saying unless the consumer, within 30 days after receipt of notice, disputes validity of the debt, or any portion thereof, the debt will be assumed to be valid by the Collector;

4) A statement that if the consumer/debtor notifies the Collector in writing within the 30-day period that the debt or any portion thereof is disputed, the Collector will obtain verification of the debt or a copy of the judgment against the consumer/debtor and a copy will be mailed to the consumer/debtor by the Collector;

21

STOP IT!

5) Upon written request provide to the consumer/debtor within 30 days the name and addresses of the original creditor if different from the current creditor;

6) If the consumer/debtor notifies the Collector, in writing (U.S. Certified Mail-Return Receipt Requested) within the 30-day period, that the debt or any portion thereof is disputed, or the consumer/debtor requests the name and address of the original creditor, the Collector shall cease collection of the debt or any disputed portion thereof until the Collector verifies the debt;

7) If a consumer/debtor fails to dispute the validity of a debt, it may not be construed by any court as an admission of liability by the consumer/debtor.

SIMPLY RESTATED: This portion of the law outlines your rights to verify and validate or dispute any debts with defined time periods.

Chapter IX

MULTIPLE DEBTS

"I'd like to live like a poor man with lots of money."
- Pablo Picasso

If any consumer/debtor owes multiple debts and makes any single payment to a Collector with respect to such debts, such Collector may not apply payment to any debt which is disputed by the consumer/debtor and, where applicable, shall apply such payment in accordance with the consumer/debtor's directions.

SIMPLY RESTATED: If you do pay a Debt Collector and that Collector is trying to collect several debts, the Collector is obliged to follow your instructions as to how your repayment is applied to the outstanding balances.

Chapter X

LEGAL ACTIONS BY DEBT COLLECTORS

"Truman's Law: If you can't convince them, confuse them."
- Harry S. Truman

A Collector who brings any legal action on a debt against a consumer/debtor shall:

1) Bring legal action against real property only in a judicial district or similar legal entity where the property is located;

2) In the case of an action not described above, bring such action only in the judicial district or similar legal entity:
   a) where the consumer/debtor signed the contract; or
   b) where the consumer/debtor resides at the commencement of the action;

3) Nothing in this title shall be construed to authorize the bringing of legal action by Debt Collectors.

SIMPLY RESTATED: An example of this part of the law: You live in Los Angeles and default on a loan made in Los Angeles and the creditor assigns your loan to a Debt Collector or other third-party (sells the note in a loan portfolio) that operates in New York. They cannot sue you and force you to

STOP IT!

defend yourself in New York. They must take any legal actions against you in the city/county in which the loan was originally made or in which you (the debtor) currently live.

Chapter XI

FURNISHING DECEPTIVE FORMS

"The truth is more important than the facts."
- Frank Lloyd Wright

It is unlawful to design, compile and furnish any form knowing such form would be used to create the false belief in a consumer/debtor that a person other than the creditor of such consumer/debtor is participating in the collection, or in an attempt to collect a debt such consumer allegedly owes such creditor, when in fact such person is not so participating.

SIMPLY RESTATED: On the next page you will see an actual example from a Collection Agency that violates this provision of the law. It gives a false impression to the consumer/ debtor, wouldn't you agree?

STOP IT!

- Deceptive Form Example -

<table>
<tr>
<td>

ATTORNEYS/AGENCY
From: ABC Collection Agency
P.O. Box 12345
New York, NY 10010-2345

</td>
<td>

COMPLAINANTS:
To: Mr. John Doe
7734 Willow Lane
Ft. Worth, TX 76116

</td>
</tr>
</table>

NOTICE OF AUTHORIZATION

GENTLEMEN: IN ACCORDANCE WITH ARRANGEMENTS PREVIOUSLY MADE, YOU ARE HEREBY DIRECTED TO TAKE ALL STEPS, INCLUDING LEGAL AGAINST THE FOLLOWING NAMED DEBTOR TO EFFECT PAYMENT OF ACCOUNT PAST DUE:

Acct: #123-456-789, ACME Department Stores, Inc.

IN THE AMOUNT OF
$354.56

PLUS ALL ALLOWANCE ACCRUED COSTS. FEES, INTEREST AND CHARGES

FOR THE FOLLOWING ITEMS OR SERVICES	ACCT /INV. NO	DATE	AMOUNT
1. Balance due on ACME Department Stores revolving charge account	#123-456-789	1-31-92	$354 56
2.			

PREVIOUS EFFORTS TO EFFECT PAYMENT HAVE BEEN AS FOLLOWS:

Demand letters mailed first class postage on 10-31-91, 11-30-91, 12-31-91

FOLD

LEGAL ACTION WILL BE RECOMENDED ON 3-15-92 UNLESS PAYMENT IS RECEIVED BEFORE THIS DATE ALL ALLOWABLE ACCRUED COSTS, FEES, INTEREST AND CHARGES TO BE ADDED TO JUDGEMENT

Richard Head, Sr. VP
COPY TO ACME Department Stores
(DEBTOR)

Dewey, Cheatham & Howe, Attys. for
COMPANY ABC Collections

WE REGRET THE NECESSITY OF THIS ACTION, BUT ALL OTHER EFFORTS HAVING FAILED, PROCEEDINGS WILL BE RECOMMENDED AUTOMATICALLY UNLESS PAYMENT IS RECEIVED

SIGNED _Steven Howe_ CREDIT DEPT

ON OR BEFORE March 15, 1992

DATE OF
AUTHORIZATION February 13, 1992

This is an attempt to collect a debt and any information obtained will be used for that purpose.

Chapter XII

CIVIL LIABILITY

"Lawyers spend a great deal of their time shoveling smoke."
- Oliver Wendell Holmes

A Debt Collector may be sued for damages for failing to comply with the Fair Debt Collection Practices Act and is liable to such a person in an amount equal to the sum of:

a) the actual damages sustained;

b) in the case of any action by an individual, such additional damages as the court may allow, but not exceeding $1,000; or

c) in the case of a class action, a minimum individual recovery not to exceed the lesser of $500,000 or 1% of the net worth of the debt collector (see Section 813 in Appendix A for full disclosures of liability).

Enforcement of this law is handled by the Federal Trade Commission.

SIMPLY RESTATED: Do not be afraid of filing any complaints you feel are justified. This law was specifically enacted to protect you, the consumer. If the Debt Collector

STOP IT!

violates your rights covered by this law and outlined in this book, you have every right to take legal action against them.

This law is useless unless **YOU** make sure it is enforced.

Chapter XIII

HOW TO ENACT THE LAW

"In matters of principle, stand like a rock; in matters of taste, swim with the current."
- Thomas Jefferson (1743-1826)

Public Law 95-109, the Fair Debt Collection Practices Act, can be invoked by anyone at anytime.

In order to utilize this federal law to effectively and legally end all Collection Agency activity, you will need the following (one set of supplies/documents per debt per Collection Agency):

1) A plain, white letter-sized envelope (ask for a #10 size from any office supply store);

2) A Cease & Desist (C&D) Letter (supplied in Appendix C in the back of this book);

3) Two forms from the U.S. Post Office (copies located in Appendices E & F):
   a) a Certified Mail Receipt (green and white), U.S. Postal Service Form #3800; and

STOP IT!

b) a Domestic Return Receipt (green card), U.S. Postal Service Form #3811;

4) Money to cover postage for mailing this letter to the Collection Agency as of December 1991 is $2.29, but is subject to any future U.S. Postal Service increases in postage;

5) The following information from the Collection Agency:
  a) the name of the account representative, the name of the Collection Agency, full mailing address (always send to a post office box, if available);
  b) the name of the creditor, account number and amount owed; and
  c) the account number assigned to you by the Collection Agency (this will help the Agency identify your account faster).

*** IMPORTANT *** IMPORTANT ***

6) Follow these directions carefully:
  a) keep the original copy of the letter sent to you by the Collection Agency (try to keep from writing on the original letter);
  b) make a copy of this original letter sent to you by the Collection Agency and enclose this with your Cease & Desist letter;
  c) make sure you keep a copy of everything you send to the Collection Agency, attaching the receipt the Post Office gives you after mailing and paying for the Certified/ Return Receipt Letter;
  d) depending on the destination of your letter to the Collection Agency, it can take anywhere from two days

32

(for a local agency) to 14 days (cross country) for you to receive the Domestic Return Receipt (green card). This card is extremely important: it is your sole proof that the Collection Agency has been duly noticed with your Cease & Desist Order. Make sure you keep the green card with all of the other documents outlined in steps 6 a-c.

PLEASE NOTE: If you do not receive this green reply card within 14 days of mailing your letter, notify your postal clerk at the Post Office from which you mailed your letter. Be sure to take all of your documents to show to the clerk, as they will need to get information from your copies and receipts. They will follow up with a tracer (U.S. Postal Service Form 3811-A): a secondary reply card (yellow) that will suffice in the event the original green card fails to be returned properly (see Appendix G).

Chapter XIV

THE CEASE & DESIST LETTER

"Leadership is action, not position."
- Donald H. McGannon

No typewriter? No problem.

Don't worry about how this letter looks. If you have to write in longhand on yellow legal paper or lined binder paper, it's okay.

The most important point is that you send the letter properly, via Certified Mail/Return Receipt Requested, as outlined on page 95 of this book. Don't cut corners: spend the few dollars per letter to send it **EXACTLY** as instructed. Only this special handling method is recognized in order to be binding. Before proceeding any further, stop by your local Post Office and pick up some of the blank forms you will need *prior* to typing your Cease & Desist letters to the Collection Agencies (all of these forms are outlined in the *"How To Enact The Law"* section, paragraph 3 a-b).

To assist you further, two options are included to help you through this. The first is located in Appendix B in the back of this book. It is a sample Cease & Desist letter format for you to follow. Be sure to change the names, addresses and other

STOP IT!

pertinent information to fit your particular case. Retype this letter, including all of the information for your own specific case.

Your next option is to review the blank letter format located in Appendix C. My suggestion is to visit your local Kwik Kopy, AlphaGraphics or other competent neighborhood printer. Ask them to carefully remove this blank format page for your book. They should have photocopiers at their store to enlarge originals. Ask them to "blow it up" several times (making sure they trim off the part at the top of the page that reads: "Appendix C, Cease & Desist Letter Blank") until it reaches approximate normal letter proportions. Then fill in the blanks with all appropriate information, including the Certified Mail receipt number across the top of the letter (as shown in Appendix B).

Chapter XV

DEALING WITH THE COLLECTION AGENCY

"Style is effectiveness of assertion."
- George Bernard Shaw

Probably the most important point to remember when dealing with any Collection Agency: you do not have to give them *ANY* information if you do not wish to. You always have the option of hanging up. You are not obligated to speak with a Collection Agency under *ANY* circumstances.

Here are some tips to follow:

DO get the Collector to identify him/herself, their company name, address and telephone number (so you can call them back). This is essential information, especially if they should be calling you at work.

Again, this is important information you need to obtain for the record.

DO ask the Collector to send you something via mail. This will give you all of the necessary information you'll need in order to send them a Cease & Desist letter.

STOP IT!

DO act cordial, but distant...even noncommittal. Remember, you are under no obligation to supply *ANY* information to a Debt Collector.

DO go by your local Radio Shack and buy an item called a "Telephone Recording Device." It retails for about $15 and plugs in-line between your telephone wall plug and a tape recorder. It is an invaluable tool to use to record conversations with Debt Collectors who choose to take the low road and threaten or annoy you. In most states, it is absolutely *LEGAL* to record a telephone conversation without notifying the other party you are doing so. The law usually states it is lawful to tape record any telephone conversation as long as *one* of the parties being recorded knows the conversation is being taped (since you are one of the parties, this makes your recording **LEGAL!**).

It is absolutely amazing how much leverage you give yourself after a few taped conversations. Not only does it help you make a case against the Collection Agency (and creditor who has employed them to collect the debt) in the event the Collector violates any of the laws outlined in this book, it also gives you more confidence, knowing you've got this person on tape in the event they start to annoy, abuse, threaten or harass you. Once you decide you've had enough and have legally notified the Debt Collector/Agency that you have decided to *"invoke the law,"* this tape will be tremendously helpful in shutting them down.

DON'T EVER, EVER, EVER sign for a Certified Letter.

Why?

38

Dealing With The Collection Agency

One of two reasons: it's from either a Collection Agency or an attorney representing a Collection Agency. If you sign for the letter, it will legally obligate you to perform in some manner by a certain date which they have determined to fit their schedule, not yours. That's why they're sending it Certified (sound familiar?). Once again, don't ever sign for a Certified Letter. Just as important, be sure to inform your spouse, roommate, children or anyone who will either pick up your mail from a post office box or answer the door when the mailman tries to deliver the letter. If the mailman should catch you in front of your residence, refuse to sign for it. He'll mark it and return it to the sender.

DON'T get into a defensive conversation with the Collector over the phone, such as, "I can't send you any money until the next payday," and don't start telling them anything about your personal life.

Why?

First, it's none of their damned business and, second, they'll use whatever you tell them against you in a later conversation. Just hang up on them. If they call back again, hang up again. If they're stupid enough to keep calling (and most of them are), keep hanging up. **It works.**

DON'T ever, *ever* send anyone a postdated check. Most people make the mistake of doing it to either "buy time" or to get the Collector off their back. It's a mistake. If you have recently sent someone a postdated check, bite the bullet and call the bank to stop payment. I know stop-payment fees from

39

STOP IT!

banks are averaging $20 per check, but this is cheaper than having "Hot Check" charges being pressed against you by the District Attorney's office.

DON'T tell them you are about to invoke the law on them when they call, because you'll be tipping your hand. If absolutely necessary, tell them you are sending them a payment on your next payday, and to make sure they receive it, you intend to send it via Certified Mail. Then they'll gladly sign for your letter. They'll be disappointed to find it's not the check you had promised!

DON'T ever get into a conversation about your debts with them over the phone from your place of employment. The last thing you need to do is lose your job because of too many personal calls. And once again, never let the Collectors intimidate you. Put them on notice that you cannot receive these types of calls at work because it is against company policy, then hang up. A war of words will go nowhere, and all they will do is upset you. **Hang up!**

Chapter XVI

DEBT COLLECTORS DON'T LIE

"A lie can travel halfway around the world
while the truth is putting on its shoes."
- Mark Twain

Remember, Debt Collectors are usually hired because of their aggressive attitudes and, as outlined earlier, normally work on a commission basis.

I don't care what they tell you. Over the past seven years I have heard every type of lie and threat imaginable. Here's a sample to give you an idea of the (un)ethical standards to which they subscribe:

"If I don't receive full payment immediately, you are going for a 5-year vacation to do some time."

"If I don't receive payment by 5:00 today, I'm sending the sheriff/police over to pick you up."

"What's your boss going to say when he finds out you don't pay your bills?"

"I'll call you anytime, anywhere I want...and there's nothing you can do about it."

41

STOP IT!

"I have the authority to have you served with legal papers where you work if I don't get paid immediately."

"Either pay me now or I will screw up your credit for the next seven years."

"I promise you that if you pay me now, there will be nothing bad on your credit report."

"I think I can stop the summons server from coming over to your job on Friday if you agree to pay me right now or send me a postdated check."

"We keep an attorney on our payroll to deal with people like you."

"How does it feel to be a deadbeat? Does your boss know that you're a scumbag who doesn't pay his/her bills?"

"Why don't you borrow money from your parents? They're dead? How about your wife's parents?"

"We will collect this money no matter what you do to try to stop us."

"If you don't get this paid off by tomorrow, I'll garnishee your next paycheck."

"I'm with an attorney's office. The law doesn't apply to me."

"Where do you work now? You'd better tell me. I'll find out. I'll find out everything about you. You can make it easier on yourself if you just tell me now. Otherwise..."

Debt Collectors Don't Lie

If you have some favorite lines of your own, please send them to the address listed in the front of this book. We'd like to see them.

Chapter XVII

CREATIVE NEGOTIATIONS

"Adversity reveals genius; prosperity conceals it."
- Horace (65-8 B.C.)

Great. You've gotten the harassing creditor phone calls to stop with your trusty Cease & Desist letters.

Now what?

Reflect for a moment on the statement I made in the first part of this book: **"Knowledge is power. Use it effectively."**

Your next step is to obtain a copy of your credit report. The easiest way to do this is to write a letter to the credit reporting agency most commonly used in your part of the country. If you have been turned down for credit recently, the letter from the company which declined your credit request will name the credit agency whose report influenced their decision against you.

For your reference, here are the addresses of the three major credit reporting agencies that cover the country:

TRW
P.O. Box 749029
Dallas, TX 75374

STOP IT!

TransUnion
P.O. Box 8070
North Olmsted, OH 44070-8070

Equifax Credit Information Services
P.O. Box 740193
Atlanta, GA 30374-0193

Use the request letter format outlined in Appendix G (located in the back of this book) to obtain a free copy of your current credit report. As of Jan. 1, 1992, TRW has stated it will give consumers one free copy of their credit report per year. Expect the other credit reporting agencies to follow suit in the near future.

Another alternative is to pay the credit reporting agency a fee for a copy of your credit report. The fee varies from state to state. Call your local agency for more information.

Your last chance at getting a free report is available courtesy of the federal government. Federal guidelines state that any consumer who has been denied credit because of a bad credit report is entitled to a free copy of that report from the credit reporting agency that reported negative information.

This "turndown" notice from whichever creditor to whom you have applied will state the name and address of the credit reporting agency you need to write to. Normally it will take the credit reporting agency two-three weeks to send you a copy of your current report. However, a recent settlement of a class action lawsuit against TRW indicates that TRW will send you your credit report within four days of receipt of your request. Now you are dealing from a position of knowledge, and **knowledge is power.** *Don't forget this!*

INVOKING THE LAW

Legally, once you've notified your Collection Agencies that you are "invoking the rule" (Public Law 95-109), they can contact you only one additional time *AFTER* they have received your Cease & Desist letter (you will know they received it when you get your green Return Reply Card back in the mail).

The Collection Agency can contact you one more time after they have received your Cease & Desist letter to let you know what further action they intend to take on behalf of their client (your original creditor).

Normally, this call will be to inform you that they intend to recommend that a lawsuit be filed against you to recover all monies owed to them, plus late fees and reasonable attorney's fees (as allowed by law). They cannot keep calling to threaten you with a lawsuit if you don't pay up (commonly known as "sabre rattling").

The majority of the time, the Collection Agency will almost immediately return the entire file to the original creditor. Usually, this will be the last you will hear about this situation, except for negative remarks on your credit rating.

There are some states that grant Collection Agencies the authority to actually file lawsuits on behalf of the original creditor.

In these particular cases, you may wish to try the strategy that follows:

47

STOP IT!

CAN YOU PAY THEM?

I don't mean 100% of what you owe them (which you would have done if you had the money anyway, right?). If you have taken your creditor and their Collection Agency this far, chances are your debt is well over 120-150 days past due.

This book is directed more towards "other" creditors: credit cards, department store charge cards and medical services (doctors, hospitals, etc). These creditors are normally "unsecured" and are counting on your good character to repay your debt to them.

UNSECURED CREDITORS

Believe me, the Collection Agency would rather receive something than nothing. They have two chances of collecting this debt once it goes to a lawsuit: **SLIM** and **NONE**.

Let's face it, you've got what they want. *YOU ARE IN THE DRIVER'S SEAT.* You can dictate any and all terms of settlement *if* they are inclined to settle. They might not be...they might be stupid enough to think they will recover their money after getting a judgment. This all really depends on the amount of money you owe your creditor.

IF you have any cash available to try to *SETTLE* this debt, make a pass at your creditor, **NOT** their Collection Agency.

Explain to them that you simply don't have the cash necessary to pay them off...that you really want to try to pay them off, but you can only give them (for example) 10 cents on the

Creative Negotiations

dollar. This means that if you owe your creditor $500, your offer of 10% will end up paying them:

$$\$500 \times 10\% = \$50$$

If they say no, then tell them that's all you can afford...you wish you could pay them more.

Tell them you are going to have to borrow the money to pay them this smaller agreed settlement amount and that you cannot get any more than that. If they don't believe you, tough luck...**FOR THEM!**

You are attempting to be reasonable with them and would like to pay everything you owe. Don't go into details why you can't pay everything you owe them...frankly, it's none of their damned business!

Simply make it clear that they have two options: settle for a lesser amount or sue you.

IF you do get sued, it's not the end of the world. We'll teach you how to live through the trauma of being sued in the next chapter. The representative with which you are dealing will either accept your offer or try to get you to pay more.

Pay what you can afford and remember, you are trying to **SETTLE** this debt. If you had the money in the first place, you would have paid them off.

But you didn't, so the next best thing is to try to get them to accept this payment as **PAYMENT TO SETTLE YOUR ACCOUNT.**

STOP IT!

Make sure they give you a letter stating that by tendering this agreed settlement amount, they agree that this settles your account in full as agreed *and* that they will not report this situation negatively on your credit report, nor will they pursue any further collection or legal action (refer to Appendix J).

If the Collection Agency has already put a "Collections Account" notation on your credit report, make sure your creditor acknowledges **IN WRITING** that this/these derogatory items will be deleted upon payment of this account. Otherwise you are wasting both your time and money.

DO NOT FALL INTO THE TRAP OF FAILING TO SECURE THIS AGREEMENT IN WRITING.

Just because they agreed on the phone to accept this payment doesn't mean they actually have the authority to settle for a lesser amount.

In fact, it could be a way for them to recover *some* money and still have you on the hook for the balance. Don't let them fool you: get it in writing on the original creditor's letterhead that they agree to settle this account for a lesser amount ***BEFORE*** sending them any money.

Don't let them con you into thinking that just because you write on the front (memo section) of the check a statement such as *"PAYMENT IN FULL"* or *"AGREED SETTLEMENT"* and they cash your check that this is binding, since they accepted the check with this endorsement.

It's not.

Creative Negotiations

Get them to send to you a "Letter of Agreed Settlement" with the same basic contents of the example in Appendix J, **SIGNED** by either a fully authorized representative of the original creditor or a fully authorized representative of the creditor's Collection Agency, and then send them the negotiated settlement check via Certified Mail.

Negotiate. *Negotiate.* <u>*NEGOTIATE!*</u>

The worst thing the original creditor can say is no. If they do, you are in no worse shape than when they started harassing you for payment in full.

SECURED CREDITORS

If your creditor is secured (by an automobile, a house/other real estate or other real property), your creditor has full recourse to recover the underlying asset if you have defaulted on the terms of your loan from them. If this is the case and you are more than 120-150 days past due, the creditor is in the "driver's seat" and has every right to recover their security. If it's an automobile, they'll hire "repo men" to get back their asset. If it is a house or other "real property" (land, for instance), they will easily recover their asset through the courts by foreclosing, the process of legally taking back an asset through the courts. You won't have the chance to try to "deal" or negotiate with creditors in these positions: they have their leverage and will rarely, if ever, waste any time with Collection Agencies.

STOP IT!

They'll simply send you the necessary demand letters and, if you don't work out your financial deficiency with the creditor, they'll seize the asset through repossession or foreclosure. You may not remember reading this, but chances are very good that you agreed to allow them this repossession/foreclosure option in the event of your default when you signed the original purchase contract.

WORK OUT FAVORABLE TERMS

Always try to work out revised repayment terms with any secured creditor, unless of course you simply cannot continue to pay for the asset they have loaned against. If you can't pay the loan/lease payments on your car, get all of your personal contents out of the auto and end the agony: tell them to come pick it up. It's far easier in the long run to turn the car over instead of playing "cat and mouse" and hiding the car in your friend's garage. The repo men will get the car sooner or later. Don't waste any more money on the car if you can't afford it (there are two types of "repos": Standard and Voluntary. It doesn't matter which one you fall victim to...a repo is a repo on your credit report).

Save what you are sending them to go towards a decent (and hopefully reliable) used car and insurance for that car, and take the proper measures to protect that asset (refer to Chapter XVIII, *"Getting Bulletproof"*).

If you can't afford the house payments, use a similar strategy. Save your money to go towards the necessary deposits on a rent house or apartment. Try to work with the lienholder on your house...sometimes they will take an action that allows you to deed the property back to them in lieu of going through foreclosure proceedings.

It is much easier and obviously cheaper for them to try to work with you, not against you. Don't go through the heartache of trying to dodge them when they come by for your house payment. It is no fun having to hide and turn the TV or stereo volume down when there is a knock at the front (or back) door.

If you try to work through the situation with the lienholder and explain to them you cannot afford the house payments, sometimes they will allow you to stay there and rent the property from them after deeding it back over. This helps everyone involved:

1) It saves them money they would have spent in foreclosure proceedings;

2) It gives them some positive cash flow until they are able to re-sell the house;

3) It gives you a sense of continuity and allows you to stay in the same place instead of uprooting yourself (and your family);

4) It saves you the expense and headache of moving. It is not cheap re-establishing utilities, telephone, paying deposits, etc. It is easier to stay in the same house under different terms.

Try to negotiate at least a 3-month lease (preferably a 6-month) to give you time to "get back on your feet" and find another place to live in the event the lienholder re-sells your

STOP IT!

house. In addition, if you are able to strike a deal and stay in your existing house and rent it, make sure you are making a smaller monthly rent payment.

Remember, you no longer own the house (assuming you deeded it back over), therefore you are no longer building any equity or receiving any tax write-offs at the end of the year. Make sure you get at least a 30%-50% reduction in what you were paying when you were buying the house.

Don't be afraid to negotiate with them. All they can say is "no."

Above all else, **get any and all agreements in writing.**

Chapter XVIII

GETTING BULLETPROOF

"Success is a journey, not a destination."
- Ben Sweetland

There is no law on the books anywhere in this great land of ours that mandates you be easily found. You certainly need to let family and friends know about any action you might take in order to insulate yourself from Collectors until your situation stabilizes. Here are some actions you should consider taking and will probably want to maintain even after your storm has passed.

Step One: <u>The Post Office.</u>

a) Get yourself the smallest post office box available; they are the cheapest. They charge rent on either 6-month or 1-year terms. I know money may be tight, but **do it.** It's cheap insurance to insulate yourself from further harassment.

b) Get change of address forms and immediately forward all of your mail from your residence to your new post office box.

STOP IT!

Step Two: The Telephone Company.

a) Change your phone number. Tell the phone company you want it changed <u>NOW</u>. Tell them you're getting harassing phone calls and want your number changed immediately;

b) At the same time, be sure to have them keep the number *UN*listed. Instruct them that you want the address unlisted as well;

c) Have the phone company change the mailing address on your bill to your new post office box;

d) Finally, many phone companies are now willing to place "code words" or "passwords" on your account. Use a word or name you'll easily remember, but avoid using your spouse's name, mother's maiden name, your middle name, etc. Collectors can be creative and can find this information though your credit files many times, then use it to get you.

Trust me.

Another telephone-related thought: by changing and unlisting your new telephone number, you will also neutralize any of the "crisscross" directories available in most libraries across the country. If the libraries have these directories, you can count on the Collection Agencies having their own copies as well.

Step Three: The Bank.

a) If you still have a checking account, change the address listed on your checks/account. Notify the bank of the change in person, and make this same change on your check reorder form when you run out;

Getting Bulletproof

b) The only information necessary on your checks is your name and mailing address. **DON'T** include your driver's license number, social security number or telephone number. This is *private* information, and is not to be sent around the country on the face of your checks. If needed, give it to the person requesting it when asked; they can write it on the face of the check.

Step Four: <u>Department of Motor Vehicles</u>.

a) Put in a change of address notification for your driver's license with the DMV, giving them your new mailing address (post office box). This will coincide with the new address on your checks;

b) Change the address on your automobile registration. It's easy to get a license plate run, thus leading anyone back to your residence. Head them off at the pass and let them go stake out your post office box. They'll never do it...they're too lazy.

STEP FIVE: If you have any judgements, liens or garnishments against either you or your spouse, or lawsuits pending, *read this:*

Laws vary from state to state, so be sure to check with an attorney. Many assets are attachable...many are exempt from creditor attachment.

a) Insulate yourself further by closing bank accounts and reopening at other branches (do this *after* giving post-judgment interrogatories or depositions);

STOP IT!

b) You can re-register automobiles in a friend's or relative's name (one who you obviously trust) if the car has a clear title. When you receive the "new" title, have the friend/relative who has helped you protect this asset endorse the title on the back (leaving the date blank). If there are any other forms or paperwork required when transferring title on a car (odometer statement, tax statement, etc.), have this person execute these as well. At the very least, notify the bank or whoever financed your car of your "new" address...and give them your *new* P.O. Box address;

NOTE: Make sure that your automobile insurance covers you in the event your vehicle is registered in someone elses' name.

c) Children's or family trusts are useful vehicles to protect assets. Consult with a reliable, *discreet* attorney.

Chapter XIX

AN INSIDER'S VIEW OF
COLLECTION AGENCY TACTICS

"Knowledge is power...if you know it about the right person."
- Ethel Watts Mumford

Since you've gotten through this book to the 19th chapter, chances are good that you've got some creditor problems. This isn't just one of those "casual" reading books.

If you've been under fire, you know the Collection Agencies can be downright nasty. Ruthless. *Total schmucks.*

I found it was easier to understand the opposition by getting inside their heads...by going behind the lines to see exactly what they are telling creditors about how to deal with delinquent accounts.

Before I knew it, I was behind the scenes, attending a seminar that specifically targeted medical professionals and their problem accounts. This seminar was sponsored by a well-known, well-established national credit reporting and collections company.

Heh, heh, heh. **Speak to me.**

Tell me all about how you plan to torture and torment unwitting debtors around the country.

STOP IT!

The seminar was actually very informative and a terrific insight into *"Collecting in the '90s."* As long as those people who are in the collecting profession handle themselves as professionals and stay within federal laws regarding this type of activity, fine. But when less-ethical individuals begin hammering on people who are intimidated and misinformed, that is the time to fight back!

THE TIME-VALUE OF MONEY

One of the early highlights of their seminar was the *TIME-VALUE* of money concept. In a nutshell, the general feeling in the business of collecting debts (in this case medical receivables) is that the longer the debts go without being paid, the less chance they have of being collected. Carrying this theory one step further dictates that the older an account is, the less value it has; an extremely important concept to any creditor who extends credit in the normal course of business.

In the medical receivable collection business, here's their view of this *TIME-VALUE* of money concept:

MONTHS PAST DUE	% OF LOSS	DOLLAR VALUE
3	10%	.90
4	14%	.86
5	19%	.81
6	33%	.67
1 year	55%	.45
2 years	77%	.23
3 years	85%	.15
4 years	88%	.12
5 years	*practically worthless*	

An Insider's View of Collection Agency Tactics

COLLECTION AGENCIES AND THE LAW

The next part of the seminar dealt with the same points covered in Chapters II-XIV, the Fair Debt Collection Practices Act (Public Law 95-109).

The same information I discussed earlier in the book was covered at the seminar, but from the creditor's perspective. Most Collectors will know the laws and will abide by your wishes, especially after they receive your Cease & Desist letter.

CREDITORS AND THE COURTS

Remember, if they're in the business of collecting accounts like yours, they've probably seen about every conceivable debtor situation.

Collection seminars will almost always cover the two types of bankruptcy procedures you should be concerned with:

Chapter 7-Liquidation, available to individuals, corporations and partnerships

Chapter 13-Rehabilitation (also known as "reorganization") available to wage-earning individuals only

Creditors and their collection agencies are also versed in lodging any claims they may have in the bankruptcy court in addition to small claims court procedures.

STOP IT!

YOUR CREDITORS:
BIG BROTHER WILL FIND YOU

One of the more interesting points of this seminar was the aggressive attitude towards *"skiptracing."*

First, some definitions:

SKIP: A debtor who cannot be readily located by the usual means of telephone or through the mail.

SKIPTRACING: The process of developing information about the debtor for the purpose of locating them and collecting their account.

Some facts creditors and their Collection Agencies know that we thought you should know, about skiptracing:

1) One of every five people move to a new address every year.

2) 35% to 50% of all accounts received by Collection Agencies require skiptracing.

3) Skiptracing is a necessity in order to decrease bad debt losses.

4) Skiptracing helps the creditor or their Collection Agency:
   a) Locate the debtor in order to collect;

An Insider's View of Collection Agency Tactics

b) Determine if the debtor is able to pay;
c) Determine if there are other creditors pursuing the same debtor;
d) Determine what the debtor's paying habits are; and
e) Determine the stability of the debtor's employment.

5) To what extent should the creditor pursue a "skip"?
a) Use good judgment and follow all state and federal laws;
b) Virtually every debtor can be located with sufficient time and expenditure of money;
c) *Creditors must limit the amount of time and money spent in order to keep skiptracing costs in line with the size of the debt;*
d) *Keep potential recovery in mind;* and
e) Skiptrace in order to locate someone who will pay the account, not just to gather information.

Notice 5/c-d are in italics. These are probably *THE MOST IMPORTANT* points to keep in mind. You can bet the creditor/Collection Agency is thinking about them.

TYPES OF SKIPS

There are four basic categories of "skips": the Unintentional Skip, Skips Resulting from Martial Difficulties, the Intentional Skip and Skips with Criminal Intent.

I think the names of each of these categories is self-explanatory, so I'll move on to the types of information

STOP IT!

creditors and their Collection Agencies intend to collect on their targeted debtors.

6) Location information:
   a) The debtor's place of residence;
   b) The telephone number at that place of residence; and
   c) The debtor's place of employment.
7) Information to be developed on skips:
   a) The debtor's name, including the correct and complete spelling of the debtor's full name, middle initial, junior or senior;
   b) The debtor's correct address, including correct street name, number and zip code (9-digit preferred);
   c) The debtor's former address;
   d) The debtor's place of employment, including their occupation, type of work or trade (remember, debtors tend to stay with their trade or occupation);
   e) Debtors who are members of trade unions, schoolteachers, nurses, etc., are relatively easy to find if you can locate the area to which they have skipped;
   f) Obtain information pertaining to position, length of employment, earnings, payday, etc.;
   g) If you are dealing with a former employer, quiz them to obtain any references or inquiries that have been made since the debtor has left;
   h) Concerning real estate, find out whether the debtor rents, leases or owns property;
   i) If the debtor owns real estate, check for the name of the mortgagor;
   j) If the debtor rents, obtain the landlord's name, address and telephone number;

An Insider's View of Collection Agency Tactics

k) Personal property: check for the registration of the
debtor's automobile;

l) Obtain name, address and telephone number of company
that holds any lien on the automobile;

m) Develop a list of any relatives or friends to contact;

n) Neighbors: an excellent source of information;

o) Current neighbors: When does the debtor go to work,
come home at night, what type of car do they drive, what
do they do for a living? and

p) Former neighbors: what moving van came to pick up the
furniture? Do you know any names of friends or
relatives?

8) Skiptracing by mail:

a) Remembering the guidelines discussed regarding what
Collection Agencies are authorized to use through the
mail, they are not to send any postcards or anything that
conveys the impression that the correspondence is from
a Collection Agency;

b) Post Office correction services: for a small fee ($1.00)
the Post Office will search their records and give you the
new address, if available;

c) Post Office will notify you of any address change on file
if you mail an envelope with the words *"ADDRESS
CORRECTION REQUESTED"* written on the front. This
fee (subject to change, currently 25 cents) will be
returned to sender within two weeks;

d) Returned mail: this is the first indication that a debtor
is probably a skip;

STOP IT!

e) Carefully examine all returned mail that is undeliverable for clues;

f) "Refused" written on envelope may indicate the debtor is still at that address;

g) "Not here" is typical post office wording that indicates the debtor is no longer there;

h) "Not there" was probably written by someone at that address;

i) "Moved, no forwarding address" indicates the debtor is probably a true skip;

j) "Forwarding order expired" indicates the time limit for forwarding has run out (however, still check with the post office);

k) Certified Mail/Return Receipt Requested: useful when you need to know for certain that a piece of mail has been delivered, and to verify who signed for it;

l) "Restricted Delivery": assures that target debtor receives mail; extra fee for this service;

m) "Forward": the debtor's new address (if on file) will show on the return item from the post office; and

n) "Return to sender if not delivered on first attempt": without this instruction, the target debtor will be able to claim the letter at the post office, and will also be tipped off that you are trying to reach him/her. In addition, you still would not have a certified address.

9) Skiptracing by telephone:

a) Telephone contacts are the most effective, fastest and cheapest methods;

An Insider's View of Collection Agency Tactics

b) Use good timing when contacting your informants in order to gain their maximum cooperation. Don't forget the time, place and type of person you are attempting to contact;

c) Avoid mealtimes or times that your informant might be hurrying to work;

d) Always leave a number for informants to call back;

e) Identify your informant: know who you are talking to and verify their name and address;

f) Identify yourself, stating only your name. Don't identify your employer, unless they specifically ask you to do so. If informant asks you to identify your employer, simply state the name of the original creditor (not your Collection Agency name);

g) Tell your informant you need their help. Make your requests courteous and friendly. Try to build a rapport with your informant immediately. Encourage them to respond;

h) Under Public Law 95-109, you can only contact their place of residence, place of employment or telephone number;

i) Use psychology on your informant: silently wait for them to make the next move. Wait for them to respond...be patient;

j) Listen for information and leads: analyze everything the informant says to you, since they may give you leads to other sources of information;

k) Analyze the informant's attitude: be alert for inadvertent clues, listen for inconsistencies;

l) Question your informant: your questions may help turn up more information that the informant realizes he/she

STOP IT!

knows. Limit your questions to acquisition of location
information. Be sure to phrase all of your questions in a
positive manner. Sound confident that you have the right
information;

m) Be prepared for any questions your prospective informant
may have for you: all questions from your informant
should be followed by a combination answer to their
question and a question of your own. This counter-
question will help prevent the informant from asking you
more questions. If the informant should ask, tell them
you need to contact the debtor about a business matter;

n) Close your call: as soon as you have all of the
information you want or all that you think you can get,
close the call; and

o) Don't allow time for the informant to ask you a lot of
questions.

10) Additional sources of information (updated periodically):
   a) The telephone directory;
   b) Crisscross directory: one section give a list of
      households and businesses by street name/number;
      another section gives a list of all telephone numbers on
      each exchange and tells who is assigned to each number;
      and
   c) City directory: this information is obtained by direct
      canvassing of the city by mail, phone and sometimes
      even personal calls. Most residents of the city are
      included, even those with unlisted phone numbers. City
      directories are normally divided into four sections:
      business and professional firms, name of residents and
      businesses listed alphabetically, listing of households and

An Insider's View of Collection Agency Tactics

businesses by street name, telephone numbers (in numerical order) followed by the names and addresses of the persons or businesses to whom the telephones are listed.

11) Who do you contact?
   a) Go back through your own files on the debtor;
   b) Contact their neighbors, friends or relatives;
   c) Former employers;
   d) Apartment managers or landlords;
   e) Local stores, service stations or barber/beauty shops the debtor might frequent;
   f) Social agencies; and
   g) Schools, alumni associations, PTAs, etc.

12) Public records/domain
   a) Review any divorce actions at the courthouse;
   b) Real estate contracts;
   c) Bankruptcies;
   d) Liens;
   e) Foreclosures;
   f) Declaration of homestead;
   g) Probate of estates;
   h) Building permits;
   i) Chattel mortgages;
   j) Deeds of all kinds; and
   k) Tax liens: state and federal

13) Additional research areas:
   a) Local newspapers;
   b) City, county and state maps;

69

STOP IT!

c) Social security number (analyze and identify part of country and approximate date of issue);
d) Chamber of Commerce membership directory (locate either target debtor or former/current employer);
e) Military base directories;
f) High school or college student/faculty directories;
g) Labor unions;
h) Finance companies;
i) Utility companies;
j) Credit bureaus;
k) Check with lienholder on current automobile;
l) Moving companies;
m) Phone company;
n) Real estate tax rolls;
o) Birth and death records;
p) Motor vehicle records; and
q) Criminal or civil records.

14) Armed Forces records:
a) Write to each branch of the service and ask for the address of your missing debtor;
b) Enclose a payment of $2.40 for each address requested;
c) Always include the social security number of the debtor to speed information search;
d) Include the city/town from which the debtor entered the service, if known;
e) If the branch of the service the debtor joined is unknown, try the U.S. Army first. Numerically, it is the largest branch of the service; and
f) Follow with the Navy, Air Force, Coast Guard, Marines and Merchant Marines.

Chapter XX

BANKRUPTCY...
THE LAST DITCH OPTION

"Bravery is being the only one who knows you're afraid."
- Franklin P. Jones

Over the past seven years, I have counseled hundreds of people across the country who were experiencing some type of financial difficulty. My job was to help them find their way through this predicament so they could attempt to resume a normal lifestyle.

Let's face it, nowadays you can't get a telephone installed or cable TV hooked up without someone pulling up your credit report.

One thing you'd better remember:

If anyone asks for your social security number, you can bet they're planning on pulling up your credit. A major misunderstanding among 99% of the consumers across America:

They don't need your authorization to do so.

71

STOP IT!

Let's assume that as you are reading this book, you are unemployed and your bills are beginning to really stack up. Just about every phone call you receive is from either a creditor or their Collection Agency threatening you with some kind of legal action.

You'd do just about anything to stop the harassment you and your family are being forced to endure. Finally, you pick up the newspaper to look through the classified ads one more time, and your eyes are suddenly transfixed:

> STOP CREDITOR HARASSMENT
> BANKRUPTCY: CHEAP, QUICK and
> PAINLESS! **Call now:** 555-1234

Everybody has worn you down. You're feeling trapped. There is no other way out. You place the call: "Yes, we can stop your creditors in their tracks. All we've got to do is file a Chapter 7 or Chapter 13 petition with the court and your creditors will have to deal with us and the trustee appointed by the bankruptcy court. It'll only cost you....."

Wrong!

It can be not just a 7- or 10-year mistake. It can be a mistake that will follow you around for the rest of your life.

Take this quick and easy 6-step *Yes or No* test. Answer *truthfully!*

Bankruptcy...The Last Ditch Option

1) I want to declare bankruptcy because it will stop all of the phone calls I've been receiving from Collection Agencies at home and at my job.

2) The attorney told me that since my credit is already ruined, bankruptcy will afford me a chance to start over...a fresh start.

3) I'm going to keep a few of my good credit cards and get rid of all of the rest through bankruptcy. It really won't affect me that badly.

4) I've heard you can take up to five years to pay back your creditors through bankruptcy, and it actually helps your credit because they're willing to work with you both during the bankruptcy and after it is over.

5) The attorney told me there is no other way out of my predicament except to declare bankruptcy. He said I'll be able to get credit again because I won't owe anything.

6) I've heard bankruptcy lasts only seven years and some creditors will even extend credit to me after only a year or two.

Do any of these sound familiar to *you*?

DON'T DO IT!

STOP IT!

I am against bankruptcy except in those extreme cases where it will actually help and is the only true option.

Everyone who I have dealt with that has already gone through bankruptcy agreed:

a) They'd never do it again because it was one of the biggest mistakes of their life; and

b) They wished they had known what I was telling them when they were under fire. If they knew then what they know now, they never would have taken bankruptcy.

Why?

Because those veterans of the bankruptcy court ended up being in worse shape than they were before... and it was too late to do anything about it! Their fates were sealed.

Here are some common questions asked by people thinking seriously about filing for bankruptcy:

1) "I have heard that most people file bankruptcy to halt Collection Agency and creditor harassment. They can't handle the constant pressure of phone calls at home or on the job."

Bankruptcy is not as easy as it may first seem. It's not cheap, and you won't walk out of the federal court with a clean record.

Bankruptcy...The Last Ditch Option

If you want to halt the harassment of Collection Agencies and creditors, follow the guidelines explained in this book, and stop them dead in their tracks.

2) "If I could stop my creditors or their Collection Agencies from harassing me and reach a settlement with the creditors without going through the court system, *I'd do it in a heartbeat.*"

Read this book again. You'll learn that you don't need to live with either the stigma attached to bankruptcy, or the cold fact that it will stay on your record for at least the next 7-10 years.

3) "I can keep my creditors from taking all of my assets if I file Chapter 7 or 13."

You can kiss any cash you've got goodbye and protect some of the rest, but at what price? This book is not designed to give you legal advice. It is designed to give you some tools you can put to work immediately to keep the wolves from your door. If your problems are so large that a bankruptcy is the only feasible way through your situation, then consult with a qualified bankruptcy attorney today.

However, many bankruptcies can be avoided by negotiating with the creditors involved...not their "hired gun" Collection Agencies. You'll never accomplish anything trying to deal with a Collection Agency. All they want is your money...and they want it yesterday. Once any defaulted loan (that is

STOP IT!

unsecured) goes to court and the creditor secures a judgment against you, you and your assets are at risk. Knowing how the game is played will save you time, grief and, above all else... money!

4) "My debts aren't too bad...some credit cards, a student loan, car payment and a consolidation loan from the credit union. Altogether, they don't add up to more than $28-30,000. Wouldn't bankruptcy be the easiest way out of this mess?"

Murderers, extortionists and bank embezzlers get off with sentences less than 7-10 years. Why put yourself in the hole voluntarily for at least that long?

Your bankruptcy will show up on your credit rating for at least 7-10 years. However, when you apply for credit after this period has passed, you'll notice that just about every credit information application will have a question that applies to you:

Have you ever filed for bankruptcy?

If you don't answer it correctly, you've just committed a felony. Now how long is your sentence resulting from your bankruptcy?

LET THE DUST SETTLE

Get the heat off by sending out Cease & Desist letters. Take time to let the dust settle and your nerves recover. Take a deep

Bankruptcy...The Last Ditch Option

breath and start your journey toward returning to normalcy. It won't be easy, but it won't be as bad as bankruptcy.

No matter how bad the situation seems, there is **ALWAYS** an alternative. Just keep working toward getting your personal situation straightened out, keep the essentials paid (rent, car payment, money for gas, food, medical, etc.) and everything will work out. It always does.

By the way, the good news is your credit rating can also be fixed.

Stay tuned: *"FIX IT,"* my next book on how to fix your credit report, is on the drawing boards and will be out soon. It works...and it won't cost you an arm and a leg.

"FIX IT" will show you how to take control of your own situation.

<u>Quit</u> depending on others.

Take the offensive for a change and come out of your corner _swinging!_

We'll show you how!

Chapter XXI

ADVICE FROM A PROFESSIONAL

"Old people love to give good advice;
it compensated them for their inability
to set a bad example."
- Du de Rochefoucauld
(1613-1680)

Some closing thoughts...

• Don't let a debt collector intimidate you. You should never be afraid of them; they don't have any power over you. Remember, it is a mind game they'll use to get you to pay off your debt to their company. ***Don't forget:*** these people normally work on commission.

• Again, don't ever sign for a certified letter. Be sure to inform everyone in your household about this. No one is obligated to sign for this type of special delivery if they don't want to. Incidentally, your postman could care less.

• Send the Cease & Desist letter to the Collection Agency as soon as you receive your first letter from them (if you've already received one or more letters, it's not too late to stop them from contacting you again). In many cases, if you send

STOP IT!

out your Cease & Desist letter to the Collection Agency as soon as you receive it, this will prevent the Collection Agency from ever "pulling up" your credit report.

This will prevent either:
  a) a notation that a Collection Agency has made an inquiry to your credit record; and
  b) information on your credit report showing your account has been assigned to a Collection Agency.

• As stated earlier, be sure to keep a file of all letters from the Collection Agency to you. Keep all postal receipts intact with this file; you'll need this information if you decide to take legal action against them.

• You've been lectured enough about sending your letter via Certified Mail. If you don't, you're wasting your time, the Collection Agency's time and the money you've spent on this book.

• If they call you at home or at work, be polite the first time and request they send you something in writing. Then...zap 'em!

If you have any collection letters or stories you think are in extraordinarily poor taste, please send me a copy of the letter or write me a letter about your experience. If I incorporate your letter or story in future editions of this book, I'll send you an autographed copy and a thank you (but not by Certified Mail!).

- APPENDIX A -

Public Law 95-109
Public Law 99-361

Fair Debt Collection Practices Act

Consumer Credit Protection Act
Amendments

81

STOP IT!

PUBLIC LAW 95-109—SEPT. 20, 1977

CONSUMER CREDIT PROTECTION ACT,
AMENDMENTS

FAIR DEBT COLLECTION PRACTICES ACT
As Amended by Public Law 99-361—July 9, 1986

82

APPENDIX A

PUBLIC LAW 95-109—SEPT. 20, 1977

PUBLIC LAW 95-109
95th CONGRESS

An Act

Sept. 20, 1977   To amend the Consumer Credit Protection Act to prohibit abusive
[H.R. 5294]   practices by debt collectors.

Consumer Credit   *Be it enacted by the Senate and House of Representatives of the United*
Protection Act.   *States of America in Congress assembled,* That the Consumer Credit Pro-
amendments.   tection Act (15 U.S.C. 1601 et seq.) is amended by adding at the end thereof
                     the following new title:

Fair Debt   "TITLE VIII—DEBT COLLECTION PRACTICES
Collection   "Sec.
Practices Act.   "801. Short title.
                     "802. Findings and purpose.
                     "803. Definitions.
                     "804. Acquisition of location information.
                     "805. Communication in connection with debt collection.
                     "806. Harassment or abuse.
                     "807. False or misleading representations.
                     "808. Unfair practices.
                     "809. Validation of debts.
                     "810. Multiple debts.
                     "811. Legal actions by debt collectors.
                     "812. Furnishing certain deceptive forms.
                     "813. Civil liability.
                     "814. Administrative enforcement.
                     "815. Reports to Congress by the Commission.
                     "816. Relation to State laws.
                     "817. Exemption for State regulation.
                     "818. Effective date.

15 USC 1601   "§ 801. **Short title**
note   "This title may be cited as the 'Fair Debt Collection Practices Act'.

15 USC 1692   "§ 802. **Findings and purpose**
                     "(a) There is abundant evidence of the use of abusive, deceptive, and
                unfair debt collection practices by many debt collectors. Abusive debt col-
                lection practices contribute to the number of personal bankruptcies, to
                marital instability, to the loss of jobs, and to invasions of individual
                privacy.
                     "(b) Existing laws and procedures for redressing these injuries are in-
                adequate to protect consumers.
                     "(c) Means other than misrepresentation or other abusive debt collec-
                tion practices are available for the effective collection of debts.
                     "(d) Abusive debt collection practices are carried on to a substantial
                extent in interstate commerce and through means and instrumentalities
                of such commerce. Even where abusive debt collection practices are purely
                intrastate in character, they nevertheless directly affect interstate
                commerce.

83

STOP IT!

"(e) It is the purpose of this title to eliminate abusive debt collection practices by debt collectors, to insure that those debt collectors who refrain from using abusive debt collection practices are not competitively disadvantaged, and to promote consistent State action to protect consumers against debt collection abuses.

"§ 803. Definitions

15 USC 1692a.

"As used in this title—

"(1) The term "Commission" means the Federal Trade Commission.

"(2) The term "communication" means the conveying of information regarding a debt directly or indirectly to any person through any medium.

"(3) The term "consumer" means any natural person obligated or allegedly obligated to pay any debt.

"(4) The term "creditor" means any person who offers or extends credit creating a debt or to whom a debt is owed, but such term does not include any person to the extent that he receives an assignment or transfer of a debt in default solely for the purpose of facilitating collection of such debt for another.

"(5) The term "debt" means any obligation or alleged obligation of a consumer to pay money arising out of a transaction in which the money, property, insurance, or services which are the subject of the transaction are primarily for personal, family, or household purposes, whether or not such obligation has been reduced to judgment.

"(6) The term "debt collector" means any person who uses any instrumentality of interstate commerce or the mails in any business the principal purpose of which is the collection of any debts, or who regularly collects or attempts to collect, directly or indirectly, debts owed or due or asserted to be owed or due another. Notwithstanding the exclusion provided by clause (F) of the last sentence of this paragraph, the term includes any creditor who, in the process of collecting his own debts, uses any name other than his own which would indicate that a third person is collecting or attempting to collect such debts. For the purpose of Section 808(6), such term also includes any person who uses any instrumentality of interstate commerce or the mails in any business the principal purpose of which is the enforcement of security interests. The term does not include—

"(A) any officer or employee of a creditor while, in the name of the creditor, collecting debts for such creditor;

"(B) any person while acting as a debt collector for another person, both of whom are related by common ownership or affiliated by corporated control, if the person acting as a debt collector does so only for persons to who it is so related or affiliated and if the principal business of such person is not the collection of debts;

"(C) any officer or employee of the United States or any State to the extent that collecting or attempting to collect any debt is in the performance of his official duties;

"(D) any person while serving or attempting to serve legal process on any other person in connection with the judicial enforcement of any debt;

"(E) any nonprofit organization which, at the request of consumers, performs bona fide consumer credit counseling and

84

APPENDIX A

PUBLIC LAW 95-109—SEPT. 20, 1977

assists consumers in the liquidation of their debts by receiving payments from such consumers and distributing such amounts to creditors; and

"(F) any person collecting or attempting to collect any debt owed or due or asserted to be owed or due another to the extent such activity (i) is incidental to a bona fide fiduciary obligation or a bona fide escrow arrangement; (ii) concerns a debt which was originated by such person; (iii) concerns a debt which was not in default at the time it was obtained by such person; or (iv) concerns a debt obtained by such person as a secured party in a commercial credit transaction involving the creditor.

"(7) The term "location information" means a consumer's place of abode and his telephone number at such place, or his place of employment.

"(8) The term "State" means any State, territory, or possession of the United States, the District of Columbia, the Commonwealth of Puerto Rico, or any political subdivision of any of the foregoing.

15 USC 1692b.   "§ 804. Acquisition of location information
"Any debt collector communicating with any person other than the consumer for the purpose of acquiring location information about the consumer shall—

"(1) identify himself, state that he is confirming or correcting location information concerning the consumer, and, only if expressly requested, identify his employer;

"(2) not state that such consumer owes any debt;

"(3) not communicate with any such person more than once unless requested to do so by such person or unless the debt collector reasonably believes that the earlier response of such person is erroneous or incomplete and that such person now has correct or complete location information;

"(4) not communicate by post card;

"(5) not use any language or symbol on any envelope or in the contents of any communication effected by the mails or telegram that indicates that the debt collector is in the debt collection business or that the communication relates to the collection of a debt; and

"(6) after the debt collector knows the consumer is represented by an attorney with regard to the subject debt and has knowledge of, or can readily ascertain, such attorney's name and address, not communicate with any person other than that attorney, unless the attorney fails to respond with a reasonable period of time to communication from the debt collector.

15 USC 1692c.   "§ 805 Communication in connection with debt collection
"(a) COMMUNICATION WITH THE CONSUMER GENERALLY.—Without the prior consent of the consumer given directly to the debt collector or the express permission of a court of competent jurisdiction, a debt collector may not communicate with a consumer in connection with the collection of any debt—

"(1) at any unusual time or place or a time or place known or which should be known to be inconvenient to the consumer. In the absence of knowledge of circumstances to the contrary, a debt col-

STOP IT!

lector shall assume that the convenient time for communicating with a consumer is after 8 o'clock antimeridian and before 9 o'clock postmeridian, local time at the the consumer's location;

"(2) if the debt collector knows the consumer is represented by an attorney with respect to such debt and has knowledge of, or can readily ascertain, such attorney's name and address, unless the attorney fails to respond within a reasonable period of time to a communication from the debt collector or unless the attorney consents to direct communication with the consumer; or

"(3) at the consumer's place of employment if the debt collector knows or has reason to know that the consumer's employer prohibits the consumer from receiving such communication.

"(b) COMMUNICATION WITH THIRD PARTIES.—Except as provided in section 804, without the prior consent of the consumer given directly to the debt collector, or the express permission of a court of competent jurisdiction, or as reasonably necessary to effectuate a postjudgment judicial remedy, a debt collector may not communicate, in connection with the collection of any debt, with any person other than the consumer, his attorney, a consumer reporting agency if otherwise permitted by law, the creditor, the attorney of the creditor, or the attorney of the debt collector.

"(c) CEASING COMMUNICATION.—If a consumer notifies a debt collector in writing that the consumer refuses to pay a debt or that the consumer wishes the debt collector to cease further communication with the consumer, the debt collector shall not communicate further with the consumer with respect to such debt, except—

"(1) to advise the consumer that the debt collector's further efforts are being terminated;

"(2) to notify the consumer that the debt collector or creditor may invoke specified remedies which are ordinarily invoked by such debt collector or creditor; or

"(3) where applicable, to notify the consumer that the debt collector or creditor intends to invoke a specified remedy.

If such notice from the consumer is made by mail, notification shall be complete upon receipt.

"(d) For the purpose of this section, the term "consumer" includes the consumer's spouse, parent (if the consumer is a minor), guardian, executor, or administrator.

"§ 806. Harassment or abuse   15 USC 1692d.

"A debt collector may not engage in any conduct the natural consequence of which is to harass, oppress, or abuse any person in connection with the collection of a debt. Without limiting the general application of the foregoing, the following conduct is a violation of this section:

"(1) The use or threat of use of violence or other criminal means to harm the physical person, reputation, or property of any person.

"(2) The use of obscene or profane language or language the natural consequence of which is to abuse the hearer or reader.

"(3) The publication of a list of consumers who allegedly refuse to pay debts, except to a consumer reporting agency or to persons meeting the requirements of section 603(f) or 604(3) of this Act.   15 USC 1618a, 1681b.

"(4) The advertisement for sale of any debt to coerce payment of the debt.

86

APPENDIX A

PUBLIC LAW 95-109—SEPT. 20, 1977

"(5) Causing a telephone to ring or engaging any person in telephone conversation repeatedly or continuously with intent to annoy, abuse, or harass any person at the called number.

"(6) Except as provided in section 804, the placement of telephone calls without meaningful disclosure of the caller's identity.

15 USC 1692e.   "**§ 807. False or misleading representations**

"A debt collector may not use any false, deceptive, or misleading representation or means in connection with the collection of any debt. Without limiting the general application of the foregoing, the following conduct is a violation of this section:

"(1) The false representation or implication that the debt collector is vouched for, bonded by, or affiliated with the United States or any State, including the use of any badge, uniform, or facsimile thereof.

"(2) The false representation of—

"(A) the character, amount, or legal status of any debt; or

"(B) any services rendered or compensation which may be lawfully received by any debt collector for the collection of a debt.

"(3) The false representation or implication that any individual is an attorney or that any communication is from an attorney.

"(4) The representation or implication that nonpayment of any debt will result in the arrest or imprisonment of any person or the seizure, garnishment, attachment, or sale of any property or wages of any person unless such action is lawful and the debt collector or creditor intends to take such action.

"(5) The threat to take any action that cannot legally be taken or that is not intended to be taken.

"(6) The false representation or implication that a sale, referral, or other transfer of any interest in a debt shall cause the consumer to—

"(A) lose any claim or defense to payment of the debt; or

"(B) become subject to any practice prohibited by this title.

"(7) The false representation or implication that the consumer committed any crime or other conduct in order to disgrace the consumer.

"(8) Communicating or threatening to communicate to any person credit information which is known or which should be known to be false, including the failure to communicate that a disputed debt is disputed.

"(9) The use or distribution of any written communication which simulates or is falsely represented to be a document authorized, issued, or approved by any court, official, or agency of the United States or any State, or which creates a false impression as to its source, authorization, or approval.

"(10) The use of any false representation or deceptive means to collect or attempt to collect any debt or to obtain information concerning a consumer.

"(11) Except as otherwise provided for communications to acquire location information under section 804, the failure to disclose clearly in all communications made to collect a debt or to obtain

87

STOP IT!

information about a consumer, that the debt collector is attempting to collect a debt and that any information obtained will be used for that purpose.

"(12) The false representation or implication that accounts have been turned over to innocent purchasers for value.

"(13) The false representation or implication that documents are legal process.

"(14) The use of any business, company, or organization name other than the true name of the debt collector's business, company, or organization.

"(15) The false representation or implication that documents are not legal process forms or do not require action by the consumer.

"(16) The false representation or implication that a debt collector operates or is employed by a consumer reporting agency as defined by section 603(f) of this Act.

15 USC 1681.

"§ 808. Unfair practices

15 USC 1692f.

"A debt collector may not use unfair or unconscionable means to collect or attempt to collect any debt. Without limiting the general application of the foregoing, the following conduct is a violation of this section:

"(1) The collection of any amount (including any interest, fee, charge, or expense incidental to the principal obligation) unless such amount is expressly authorized by the agreement creating the debt or permitted by law.

"(2) The acceptance by a debt collector from any person of a check or other payment instrument postdated by more than five days unless such person is notified in writing of the debt collector's intent to deposit such check or instrument not more than ten nor less than three business days prior to such deposit.

"(3) The solicitation by a debt collector of any postdated check or other postdated payment instrument for the purpose of threatening or instituting criminal prosecution.

"(4) Depositing or threatening to deposit any postdated check or other postdated payment instrument prior to the date on such check or instrument.

"(5) Causing charges to be made to any person for communications by concealment of the true purpose of the communication. Such charges include, but are not limited to, collect telephone calls and telegram fees.

"(6) Taking or threatening to take any nonjudicial action to effect dispossession or disablement of property if—

"(A) there is no present right to possession of the property claimed as collateral through an enforceable security interest;

"(B) there is no present intention to take possession of the property; or

"(C) the property is exempt by law from such dispossession or disablement.

"(7) Communicating with a consumer regarding a debt by post card.

"(8) Using any language or symbol, other than the debt collector's address, on any envelope when communicating with a con-

88

APPENDIX A

sumer by use of the mails or by telegram, except that a debt collector may use his business name if such name does not indicate that he is in the debt collection business.

15 USC 1692g.

"§ 809. Validation of debts
"(a) Within five days after the initial communication with a consumer in connection with the collection of any debt, a debt collector shall, unless the following information is contained in the initial communication or the consumer has paid the debt, send the consumer a written notice containing—
    "(1) the amount of the debt;
    "(2) the name of the creditor to whom the debt is owed;
    "(3) a statement that unless the consumer, within thirty days after receipt of notice, disputes the validity of the debt, or any portion thereof, the debt will be assumed to be valid by the debt collector;
    "(4) a statement that if the consumer notifies the debt collector in writing within the thirty-day period that the debt, or any portion thereof, is disputed, the debt collector will obtain verification of the debt or a copy of a judgment against the consumer and a copy of such verification or judgment will be mailed to the consumer by the debt collector; and
    "(5) a statement that, upon the consumer's written request within the thirty-day period, the debt collector will provide the consumer with the name and address of the original creditor, if different from the current creditor.
"(b) If the consumer notifies the debt collector in writing within the thirty-day period described in subsection (a) that the debt, or any portion thereof, is disputed, or that the consumer requests the name and address of the original creditor, the debt collector shall cease collection of the debt, or any disputed portion thereof, until the debt collector obtains verification of the debt or a copy of a judgment, or the name and address of the original creditor, and a copy of such verification or judgment, or name and address of the original creditor, is mailed to the consumer by the debt collector.
"(c) The failure of a consumer to dispute the validity of a debt under this section may not be construed by any court as an admission of liability by the consumer.

15 USC 1692h.

"§ 810. Multiple debts
"If any consumer owes multiple debts and makes any single payment to any debt collector with respect to such debts, such debt collector may not apply such payment to any debt which is disputed by the consumer and, where applicable, shall apply such payment in accordance with the consumer's directions.

15 USC 1692i.

"§ 811. Legal actions by debt collectors
"(a) Any debt collector who brings any legal action on a debt against any consumer shall—
    "(1) in the case of an action to enforce an interest in real property securing the consumer's obligation, bring such action only in a judicial district or similar legal entity in which such real property is located; or
    "(2) in the case of an action not described in paragraph (1), bring such action only in the judicial district or similar legal entity—

89

STOP IT!

"(A) in which such consumer signed the contract sued upon; or

"(B) in which such consumer resides at the commencement of the action.

"(b) Nothing in this title shall be construed to authorize the bringing of legal actions by debt collectors.

"**§ 812. Furnishing certain deceptive forms.**   15 USC 1692j.

"(a) It is unlawful to design, compile, and furnish any form knowing that such form would be used to create the false belief in a consumer that a person other than the creditor of such consumer is participating in the collection of or in an attempt to collect a debt such consumer allegedly owes such creditor, when in fact such person is not so participating.

"(b) Any person who violates this section shall be liable to the same extent and the same manner as a debt collector is liable under section 813 for failure to comply with a provision of this title.

"**§ 813. Civil liability**   15 USC 1692k.

"(a) Except as otherwise provided by this section, any debt collector who fails to comply with any provision of this title with respect to any person is liable to such person in an amount equal to the sum of—

"(1) any actual damage sustained by such as a result of such failure;

"(2) (A) in the case of any action by an individual, such additional damages as the court may allow, but not exceeding $1,000; or

"(B) in the case of a class action, (i) such amount for each named plaintiff as could be recovered under subparagraph (A), and (ii) such amount as the court may allow for all other class members, without regard to a minimum individual recovery, not to exceed the lesser of $500,000 or 1 per centum of the net worth of the debt collector; and

"(3) in the case of any successful action to enforce the foregoing liability, the costs of the action, together with a reasonable attorney's fee as determined by the court. On a finding by the court that an action under this section was brought in bad faith and for the purpose of harassment, the court may award to the defendant attorney's fees reasonable in relation to the work expended and costs.

"(b) In determining the amount of liability in any action under subsection (a), the court shall consider, among other relevant factors—

"(1) in any individual action under subsection (a)(2)(A), the frequency and persistence of noncompliance by the debt collector, the nature of such noncompliance, and the extent to which such noncompliance was intentional; or

"(2) in any class action under subsection (a)(2)(B), the frequency and persistence of noncompliance by the debt collector, the nature of such noncompliance, the resources of the debt collector, the number of persons adversely affected, and the extent to which the debt collector's noncompliance was intentional.

"(c) A debt collector may not be held liable in any action brought under this title if the debt collector shows by a preponderance of evidence that the violation was not intentional and resulted from a bona

90

APPENDIX A

PUBLIC LAW 95-109—SEPT. 20, 1977

fide error notwithstanding the maintenance of procedures reasonably adapted to avoid any such error.

Jurisdiction   "(d) An action to enforce any liability created by this title may be brought in any appropriate United States district court without regard to the amount in controversy, or in any other court of competent jurisdiction, within one year from the date on which the violation occurs.

"(e) No provision of this section imposing any liability shall apply to any act done or omitted in good faith in conformity with any advisory opinion of the Commission, not withstanding that after such act or omission has ocurred, such opinion is amended, rescinded, or determined by judicial or other authority to be invalid for any reason.

15 USC 1692l.   **"§ 814. Administrative enforcement**

"(a) Compliance with this title shall be enforced by the Commission, except to the extent that enforcement of the requirements imposed under this title is specifically committed to another agency under subsection (b). For purpose of the exercise by the Commission of its functions and powers under the Federal Trade Commission Act, a violation of this title shall be deemed an unfair or deceptive act or practice in violation of that Act. All of the functions and powers of the Com-

15 USC 58.   mission under the Federal Trade Commission Act are available to the Commission to enforce compliance by any person with this title, irrespective of whether that person is engaged in commerce or meets any other jurisdictional tests in the Federal Trade Commission Act, including the power to enforce the provisions of this title in the same manner as if the violation had been violation of a Federal Trade Commission trade regulation rule.

"(b) Compliance with any requirement imposed under this title shall be enforced under—

15 USC 1818.   "(1) section 8 of the Federal Deposit Insurance Act, in the case of-

"(A) national banks, by the Comptroller of the Currency;
"(B) member banks of the Federal Reserve System (other than national banks), by the Federal Reserve Board; and
"(C) banks the deposits or accounts of which are insured by the Federal Deposit Insurance Corporation (other than members of the Federal Reserve System), by the Board of Directors of the Federal Deposit Insurance Corporation;

12 USC 1464.   "(2) section 5(d) of the Home Owners Loan Act of 1933, sec-
12 USC 1730.   tion 407 of the National Housing Act, and sections 6(i) and 17 of
12 USC 1426,   the Federal Home Loan Bank Act, by the Federal Home Loan Bank
1437.   Board (acting directly or through the Federal Savings and Loan Insurance Corporation), in the case of any institution subject to any of those provisions;

12 USC 1751.   "(3) the Federal Credit Union Act, by the National Credit Union Administration Board with respect to any Federal credit union;

"(4) subtitle IV of Title 49, by the Interstate Commerce Commission with respect to any common carrier subject to such subtitle;

49 USC 1301   "(5) the Federal Aviation Act of 1958, by the Secretary of
note.   Transportation with respect to any air carrier or any foreign air carrier subject to that Act; and

91

STOP IT!

"(6) the Packers and Stockyards Act, 1921 (except as provided in section 406 of that Act, by the Secretary of Agriculture with respect to any activities subject to that Act.

7 USC 181.
7 USC 226.
227.

"(c) For the purpose of the exercise by any agency referred to in subsection (b) of its powers under an Act referred to in that subsection, a violation of any requirement imposed under this title shall be deemed to be a violation of a requirement imposed under that Act. In addition to its powers under any provision of law specifically referred to in subsection (b), each of the agencies referred to in that subsection may exercise, for the purpose of enforcing compliance with any requirement imposed under this title any other authority conferred on it by law, except as provided in subsection (d).

"(d) Neither the Commission nor any other agency referred to in subsection (b) may promulgate trade regulation rules or other regulations with respect to the collection of debt collectors as defined in this title.

"§ 815. Reports to Congress by the Commission

15 USC 1692m.

"(a) Not later than one year after the effective date of this title and at one-year intervals thereafter, the Commission shall make reports to the Congress concerning the administration of its functions under this title, including such recommendations as the Commission deems necessary or appropriate. In addition, each report of the Commission shall include its assessment of the extent to which compliance with this title is being achieved and a summary of the enforcement actions taken by the Commission under section 814 of this title.

"(b) In the exercise of its functions under this title, the Commission may obtain upon request the views of any other Federal agency which exercises enforcement functions under section 814 of this title.

"§ 816. Relation to State laws

15 USC 1692n.

"This title does not annul, alter, or affect, or exempt any person subject to the provisions of this title from complying with the laws of any State with respect to debt collection practices, except to the extent that those laws are inconsistent with any provision of this title, and then only to the extent of the inconsistency. For purposes of this section, a State law is not inconsistent with this title if the protection such law affords any consumer is greater than the protection provided by this title.

"§ 817 Exemption for State regulation

15 USC 1692o.

"The Commission shall by regulation exempt from the requirements of this title any class of debt collection practices within any State if the Commission determines that under the law of that State that class of debt collection practices is subject to requirements substantially similar to those imposed by this title, and that there is adequate provision for enforcement.

"§ 818. Effective date

15 USC 1692 note.

"This title takes effect upon the expiration of six months after the date of this enactment, but section 809 shall apply only with respect

APPENDIX A

PUBLIC LAW 95-109—SEPT. 20, 1977

to debts for which the initial attempt to collect occurs after such effective date.''

Approved September 20, 1977.

LEGISLATIVE HISTORY:

Public Law 95-109 [H.R. 5294]:
HOUSE REPORT No. 95-131 (Comm. on Banking, Finance, and Urban Affairs).
SENATE REPORT No. 95-382 (Comm. on Banking, Housing, and Urban Affairs).
CONGRESSIONAL RECORD, Vol. 123 (1977):
    Apr. 4, considered and passed House.
    Aug. 5, considered and passed Senate, amended.
    Sept. 8, House agreed to Senate amendment.
WEEKLY COMPILATION OF PRESIDENTIAL DOCUMENTS, Vol. 13, No. 39:
    Sept. 20, Presidential statement.

AMENDMENTS:

SECTION 621, SUBSECTIONS (b)(3), (b)(4) and (b)(5) were amended to transfer certain administrative enforcement responsibilities pursuant to Pub. L. 95-473, § 3(b), Oct. 17, 1978. 92 Stat. 166; Pub. L. 95-630, Title V. § 501, November 10, 1978, 92 Stat. 3680; Pub. L. 98-443, § 9(h), Oct. 4, 1984, 98 Stat. (708.)

SECTION 803, SUBSECTION (6), defining "debt collector," was amended to repeal the attorney at law exemption at former Section (6)(F) and to redesignate Section 803(6)(G) pursuant to Pub. L. 99-361, July 9, 1986, 100 Stat. 768. For legislative history, see H.R. 237, HOUSE REPORT No. 99-405 (Comm. on Banking, Finance and Urban Affairs). CONGRESSIONAL RECORD: Vol. 131 (1985): Dec. 2, considered and passed House. Vol. 132 (1986): June 26, considered and passed Senate.

- APPENDIX B -

Cease & Desist Sample Letter

STOP IT!

- APPENDIX B -

Cease & Desist Sample Letter

MR. JOHN DOE
Post Office Box 9822
Fort Worth, Texas 76147-2822

VIA CERTIFIED MAIL, RETURN RECEIPT REQUESTED #P 882 597 882

February 30, 1992

ABC Collection Agency
ATTN: Mr. Tom Smith
P.O. Box 12345
New York, NY 10010-2345

RE: ACME Department Store v. John Doe, Account #123-456-789
      Amount: $354.56

Dear Mr. Smith:

This letter will serve as your legal notice under federal law that regulates the activities of collection agencies and their legal representatives.

You are hereby notified under provisions of Public Law 95-109, Section 805-C, THE FAIR DEBT COLLECTION PRACTICES ACT to hereby CEASE AND DESIST in any and all attempts to collect the above debt.

Your failure to do so WILL result in charges being filed against you with the state and federal regulatory agencies empowered with enforcement.

You are further warned that if ANY derogatory information is placed on any credit reports after receipt of this notice, it too will result in action being taken against you.

APPENDIX B

As it is my position not to recognize and/or work with collection agencies, I will settle this matter directly with the original creditor.

GIVE THIS MATTER THE ATTENTION IT DESERVES.

Yours truly,

John Doe

- APPENDIX C -

Cease & Desist Letter Blank

STOP IT!

- APPENDIX C -

Cease & Desist Letter Blank

_____

_____

_____

VIA CERTIFIED MAIL, RETURN RECEIPT REQUESTED #P_____

_____

_____

ATTN: _____

_____

_____

RE: _____

Dear _____:

This letter will serve as your legal notice under federal law that regulates the activities of collection agencies and their legal representatives.

You are hereby notified under provisions of Public Law 95-109, Section 805-C, THE FAIR DEBT COLLECTION PRACTICES ACT to hereby CEASE AND DESIST in any and all attempts to collect the above debt.

Your failure to do so WILL result in charges being filed against you with the state and federal regulatory agencies empowered with enforcement.

You are further warned that if ANY derogatory information is placed on any credit reports after receipt of this notice, it too will result in action being taken against you.

APPENDIX C

As it is my position not to recognize and/or work with collection agencies, I will settle this matter directly with the original creditor.

GIVE THIS MATTER THE ATTENTION IT DESERVES.

Yours truly,

_____

- APPENDIX D -

Facts for Consumers from
The Federal Trade Commission

- APPENDIX D -

from the Federal Trade Commission

Fair Debt Collection

If you use credit cards, owe money on a personal loan, or are paying on a home mortgage, you are a "debtor." If you fall behind in repaying your creditors, or an error is made on your accounts, you may be contacted by a "debt collector."

You should know that in either situation the Fair Debt Collection Practices Act requires that debt collectors treat you fairly by prohibiting certain methods of debt collection. Of course, the law does not forgive any legitimate debt you owe.

This fact sheet provides answers to commonly asked questions to help you understand your rights under the Fair Debt Collection Practices Act.

What debts are covered?

Personal, family, and household debts are covered under the Act. This includes money owed for the purchase of an automobile, for medical care, or for charge accounts.

Who is a debt collector?

A debt collector is any person, other than the creditor, who regularly collects debts owed to others. Under a 1986 amendment to the Fair Debt Collection Practices Act, this includes attorneys who collect debts on a regular basis.

How may a debt collector contact you?

A collector may contact you in person, by mail, telephone, telegram, or FAX. However, a debt collector may not contact you at unreasonable times or places, such as before 8 a.m. or after 9 p.m., unless you agree.

A debt collector also may not contact you at work if the collector knows that your employer disapproves.

Can you stop a debt collector from contacting you?

You may stop a collector from contacting you by writing a letter to the collection agency telling them to stop. Once the agency receives your letter, they may not contact you again except to say there will be no further contact. Another exception is that the agency may notify you if the debt collector or the creditor intends to take some specific action.

May a debt collector contact any person other than you concerning your debt?

If you have an attorney, the debt collector may not contact anyone other than your attorney. If you do not have an attorney, a collector may contact other people, but only to find out where you live and work. Collectors are usually prohibited from contacting such permissible third parties more than once. In most cases, the collector is not permitted to tell anyone other than you and your attorney that you owe money.

What is the debt collector required to tell you about the debt?

Within five days after you are first contacted, the collector must send you a written notice telling you the amount of money you owe; the name of the creditor to whom you owe the money; and what action to take if you believe you do not owe the money.

Office of Consumer/Business Education   (202) 326-3650   Bureau of Consumer Protection

APPENDIX D

May a debt collector continue to contact you if you believe you do not owe money?

A collector may not contact you if, within 30 days after you are first contacted, you send the collection agency a letter stating you do not owe money. However, a collector can renew collection activities if you are sent proof of the debt, such as a copy of a bill for the amount owed.

What types of debt collection practices are prohibited?

Harassment. Debt collectors may not harass, oppress, or abuse any person. For example, debt collectors may not:

- use threats of violence or harm against the person, property, or reputation;
- publish a list of consumers who refuse to pay their debts (except to a credit bureau);
- use obscene or profane language;
- repeatedly use the telephone to annoy someone;
- telephone people without identifying themselves;
- advertise your debt.

False statements. Debt collectors may not use any false statements when collecting a debt. For example, debt collectors may not:

- falsely imply that they are attorneys or government representatives;
- falsely imply that you have committed a crime;
- falsely represent that they operate or work for a credit bureau;
- misrepresent the amount of your debt;
- misrepresent the involvement of an attorney in collecting a debt;
- indicate that papers being sent to you are legal forms when they are not;
- indicate that papers being sent to you are not legal forms when they are.

Debt collectors also may not state that:

- you will be arrested if you do not pay your debt;
- they will seize, garnish, attach, or sell your property or wages, unless the collection agency or creditor intends to do so, and it is legal to do so;
- actions, such as a lawsuit, will be taken against you, which legally may not be taken, or which they do not intend to take.

Debt collectors may not:

- give false credit information about you to anyone;
- send you anything that looks like an official document from a court or government agency when it is not;
- use a false name.

Unfair practices. Debt collectors may not engage in unfair practices in attempting to collect a debt. For example, collectors may not:

- collect any amount greater than your debt, unless allowed by law;
- deposit a post-dated check prematurely;
- make you accept collect calls or pay for telegrams;
- take or threaten to take your property unless this can be done legally;
- contact you by postcard.

What control do you have over payment of debts?

If you owe more than one debt, any payment you make must be applied to the debt you indicate. A debt collector may not apply a payment to any debt you believe you do not owe.

What can you do if you believe a debt collector violated the law?

You have the right to sue a collector in a state or federal court within one year from the date you believe the law was violated. If you win, you may recover money for the damages you suffered. Court costs and attorney's fees also can be recovered. A group of people may also sue a debt collector and recover money for damages up to $500,000, or one percent of the collector's net worth, whichever is less.

Where can you report a debt collector for an alleged violation of the law?

Report any problems you have with a debt collector to your state Attorney General's office and the Federal Trade Commission. Many states also have their own debt collection laws and your Attorney General's office can help you determine your rights.

STOP IT!

If you have questions about the Fair Debt Collection Practices Act, or your rights under the Act, write: Federal Trade Commission, Division of Credit Practices, Washington, D.C. 20580. Although the Commission generally cannot intervene in individual disputes, the information you provide may indicate a pattern of possible law violations requiring action by the Commission.

6/79;4/80;7/82;12/86;2/88;9/91

Federal Trade Commission Headquarters

6th & Pennsylvania Avenue, N.W.
Washington, D.C. 20580
(202) 326-2222

Federal Trade Commission Regional Offices

1718 Peachtree Street, N.W.
Atlanta, Georgia 30367
(404) 347-4836

10 Causeway Street
Boston, Massachusetts 02222
(617) 565-7240

55 East Monroe Street
Chicago, Illinois 60603
(312) 353-4423

668 Euclid Avenue
Cleveland, Ohio 44114
(216) 522-4207

100 N. Central Expressway
Dallas, Texas 75201
(214) 767-5501

1405 Curtis Street
Denver, Colorado 80202
(303) 209-2271

11000 Wilshire Boulevard
Los Angeles, California 90024
(213) 575-7575

150 Williams Street
New York, New York 10038
(212) 264-1207

901 Market Street
San Francisco, California 94103
(415) 744-7920

915 Second Avenue
Seattle, Washington 98174
(206) 553-4656

- APPENDIX E -

**How to Correctly Complete
U.S. Post Office Form #3800**

STOP IT!

- APPENDIX E -

How To Correctly Complete
U.S. Post Office Form #3800

STEP ONE: Fill in the first line (a) with the name of the Collection Agency.

STEP TWO: Fill in the second line (b) with the street or mailing address of the Collection Agency.

STEP THREE: Fill in the third line (c) with the city, state and zip code of the Collection Agency.

STEP FOUR: Moisten the green label (bottom half) of the form and attach directly to the right of your return address (making sure you do not cover your return address).

The Post Office will fill out the rest of the form after you have paid them the appropriate fee.

U.S. Postal Service Form #3800

- EXAMPLE -

P 882 597 882

Certified Mail Receipt
No Insurance Coverage Provided
Do not use for International Mail
(See Reverse)

UNITED STATES
POSTAL SERVICE

Sent to
ABC Collection Agency

Street & No.
P.O. Box 12345

P.O., State & ZIP Code
New York, NY 10010-2345

Postage	$
Certified Fee	
Special Delivery Fee	
Restricted Delivery Fee	
Return Receipt Showing to Whom & Date Delivered	
Return Receipt Showing to Whom, Date, & Address of Delivery	
TOTAL Postage & Fees	$
Postmark or Date	

PS Form 3800, June 1990

Fold at line over top of envelope to the right of the return address.

CERTIFIED

P 882 597 882

MAIL

109

- APPENDIX F -

**How To Correctly Complete
U.S. Post Office Form #3811
(Green Return Reply/Receipt Card)**

STOP IT!

- APPENDIX F -

How To Correctly Complete
U.S. Post Office Form #3811
(Green Return Reply/Receipt Card)

STEP ONE: Fill in your complete _NEW_ address (a) (it's a post office box by now, right?).

STEP TWO: In section 3, fill in the name of the Collection Agency and name of the representative to which your letter is addressed. Be sure to include their zip code.

APPENDIX F

STEP THREE: In section 4a, fill in the number from U.S. Post Office Form #3800 (see Appendix E). Remember, this number should also be printed across the top of the letter being sent to the Collection Agency and representative.

SENDER:
- Complete items 1 and/or 2 for additional services.
- Complete items 3, and 4a & b.
- Print your name and address on the reverse of this form so that we can return this card to you.
- Attach this form to the front of the mailpiece, or on the back if space does not permit.
- Write "Return Receipt Requested" on the mailpiece below the article number.
- The Return Receipt Fee will provide you the signature of the person delivered to and the date of delivery.

I also wish to receive the following services (for an extra fee):
1. ☐ Addressee's Address
2. ☐ Restricted Delivery

Consult postmaster for fee.

3. Article Addressed to:

ABC Collection Agency
ATTN: Mr. Tom Smith
P.O. Box 12345
New York, NY 10010-2345

4a. Article Number
P 882 597 882

4b. Service Type
☐ Registered ☐ Insured
☒ Certified ☐ COD
☐ Express Mail ☐ Return Receipt for Merchandise

7. Date of Delivery

5. Signature (Addressee)

8. Addressee's Address (Only if requested and fee is paid)

6. Signature (Agent)

PS Form **3811**, November 1990 ☆U.S. GPO: 1991—287-066 **DOMESTIC RETURN RECEIPT**

STEP FOUR: In section 4b, mark the box with the word "Certified" next to it.

All of the other lines should be left blank. They will be filled in by the mail carrier delivering the letter to the Collection Agency and representative.

- APPENDIX G -

**How To Correctly Complete
U.S. Post Office Form #3811-A
(Yellow Reply Card Tracer)**

- APPENDIX G -

How To Correctly Complete
U.S. Post Office Form #3811-A
(Yellow Reply Card Tracer)

Remember, this card is only filled out when it is apparent your green reply receipt card has been lost. Be sure to allow 14 days for the return of the green card.

Be sure to have all of your receipts from when you originally mailed the letter. You should have attached to your file copy of the letter you mailed the white half of U.S. Post Office Form #3800. When you mailed your letter, the Post Office filled in this part of the form, showing which services you requested and paid for, along with their postmark. This will give the postal clerk ample evidence to send this yellow tracer card through the system.

STEP ONE: Fill in your name and the same mailing/return address you wrote on the green card (a).

APPENDIX G

STEP TWO: Fill in your city, state and zip code on this line (b). This will make sure this card is returned to your post office branch.

UNITED STATES POSTAL SERVICE
OFFICIAL BUSINESS

RETURN TO (Enter name and address of customer making inquiry)

JOHN DOE
NAME P.O. BOX 9822
STREET
FT. WORTH TX 76147-2822
CITY   STATE   ZIP CODE

U.S. MAIL

PENALTY FOR PRIVATE
USE, $300

TO: POSTMASTER

FT. WORTH TX 76147
CITY   STATE   ZIP CODE

DELIVERY OFFICE: *(After completion—cross out Postmaster's address and return to customer shown in return address)*

117

STOP IT!

STEP THREE: Fill in the date you mailed your original letter on line 3. Use the date of the postmark on the white half of U.S. Postal Service Form #3800.

STEP FOUR: Fill in the "Certified No." of the letter you originally mailed on line 6. This number will be the same one printed at the top of the white half of U.S. Postal Service Form #3800 (referred to above).

APPENDIX G

STEP FIVE: Fill in the name and address of the Collection Agency where you sent your original letter on line 9. This name and address should match the one written on the white half of U.S. Postal Service Form #3800.

The postal clerk will handle the rest of the lines. You should receive this card within 14 days from the date you put in the tracer card.

- APPENDIX H -

SAMPLE REQUEST LETTER
FOR COPY OF CREDIT REPORT

STOP IT!

- APPENDIX H -

SAMPLE REQUEST LETTER
FOR COPY OF CREDIT REPORT

JOHN DOE
Post Office Box 9822
Fort Worth, Texas 76147-2822

February 30, 1992

TRW Credit Data
12606 Greenville Avenue
Dallas, TX 75374

RE: ACME Department Store reference #123-456-789

To Whom It May Concern:

Pursuant to federal laws, please let this letter serve as my official request for a current copy of my credit file as a result of my recently being declined for credit by ACME Department Store.

My social security number is: 123-45-6789.

Please forward a copy of this report to my mailing address listed above.

Thank you for your prompt attention to this matter.

Sincerely,

John Doe

- APPENDIX I -

**BLANK LETTER FORMAT
USED TO REQUEST A
CURRENT COPY OF CREDIT REPORT**

STOP IT!

- APPENDIX I -

BLANK LETTER FORMAT
USED TO REQUEST A
CURRENT COPY OF CREDIT REPORT

_____

_____

_____

_____

_____

_____

_____

RE:_____

To Whom It May Concern:

Pursuant to federal laws, please let this letter serve as my official request for a current copy of my credit file as a result of my recently being declined for credit by _____.

My social security number is:_____.

Please forward a copy of this report to my mailing address listed above.

Thank you for your prompt attention to this matter.

Sincerely,

_____

- APPENDIX J -

**SAMPLE LETTER FORMAT
UTILIZED TO SETTLE AN
OUTSTANDING BALANCE WITH A CREDITOR**

STOP IT!

- APPENDIX J -

SAMPLE LETTER FORMAT
UTILIZED TO SETTLE AN
OUTSTANDING BALANCE WITH A CREDITOR

MR. JOHN DOE
Post Office Box 9822
Fort Worth, Texas 76147-2822

VIA CERTIFIED MAIL, RETURN RECEIPT REQUESTED #P 123 456 789

February 30, 1992

Mr. Richard Head
Vice President of Financial Services
ACME Department Store
1234 Disk Drive
Los Angeles, CA 90010-1234

RE: Agreed settlement of outstanding balance of $725.00 on account #123-456

Dear Mr. Head:

As we have discussed via telephone on several occasions over the last few months, I am willing to settle the outstanding balance on my account referenced above.

By affixing your signature on this letter of settlement/agreement, you agree on behalf of ACME Department Stores, Inc. to the following:

APPENDIX J

1) You agree to accept the enclosed money order in the amount of $72.50 as an agreed settlement of all outstanding charges/fees on the account referenced above;

2) You agree to cease any and all attempts to collect this debt, either directly or through a Collection Agency;

3) You agree not to sell this debt to any third party since you now recognize this account to be "SETTLED AS AGREED";

4) You agree to retract all negative or derogatory remarks you may have reported on my credit report with any credit reporting agency located in the United States.

Please sign and return a copy of the letter enclosed in the attached pre-addressed/ postage paid envelope.

Thank you for your cooperation in this matter.

Sincerely,   ACCEPTED AND AGREED TO:

John Doe   Richard Head   Date

GLOSSARY

Accounts Receivable: Term used for credit extended by any person or company to another normally unsecured, with usual repayment terms requiring a monthly payment to amortize the balance owed.

Amortize: To liquidate or reduce an amount owed through a series of payments.

Attorney: A legal agent authorized to appear before a court of law as a representative of a party to a legal controversy.

Bad Debt Expense: An accounting category reserved for debts deemed uncollectible.

Blackmail: Any payment induced by or through intimidation, by use of threats of injurious information or accusations.

Certified Mail: Specialized postal service technique utilized to track delivery and obtain proof of delivery of letters or packages.

Clear automobile titles: An automobile (or other motor vehicle) that does not have a lien in place by a lender, making it free of debt and fully negotiable.

Coercion: Exercising force to obtain compliance.

STOP IT!

Commission: A sum or percentage paid to a person for his successful completion of services.

Contingency Basis: A fee paid to a third party for their involvement in either a legal proceeding or debt collection. This fee is normally paid only when a successful outcome to a legal proceeding or debt has been collected, either in part or in full.

Credit record: National grading system filed by subject's name, birth date and social security number. Major companies providing these services include TRW, TransUnion and Equifax.

Deep Discounts: Selling Accounts Receivable or Bad Debts at an amount normally less than 50% of the outstanding balance.

Depositions: Sworn statements made in the presence of a court reporter (usually) as a result of questions posed by attorneys in court (or post judgment) action. These statements are normally made outside a court of law, but are fully admissible during trial and fully binding under perjury statutes.

Disablement of property: Usually associated with motor vehicles, techniques in this area include placing locking mechanisms on wheels, disconnecting or locking steering mechanisms, disconnecting battery cables to keep the vehicle from starting, etc.

Discounts: Selling Accounts Receivable or Bad Debts at an amount normally in excess of 51% of the outstanding balance.

Glossary

Dispossession of property: Taking away property against the owner's wishes, normally as a result of non-payment.

Exempt assets: Assets not at risk of being seized or forfeited as a result of legal action.

Getting bulletproof: Term used to describe process to insulate a person from lawsuits, garnishments, creditor intrusion and harassment. Popularized in Texas during the late 1980s.

Hot checks: Drafts on a bank account that will be or have been returned by the bank for insufficient funds to pay face amount of check issued.

Interrogatories: Sworn statements made in writing as a result of a list of questions/inquiries by attorneys in court (or post judgment) action.

Intimidation: Inspiring or inducing fear.

Lawyers: *See* Attorneys.

Negative remarks: Statements or grades assigned on credit reports due to late payment, non-payment or default on debts owed to creditors. Bankruptcies and liens also show up under this category.

Postdated checks: A check with a date in the future, a technique utilized to commit a person to make payment after the date written on the check.

131

STOP IT!

Profit & Loss Statement: A timely accounting function that shows a reconciliation of all gross income and expenses to offset the same, arriving at a net profit (or loss) figure.

Regulatory agencies: Any agency empowered by either local, state or federal authorities to enforce civil laws.

Reply card tracer: Used by Postal Service to track down return receipts that never returned to verify delivery of parcel.

Return receipts: Work in conjunction with Certified Mail, receipts (green card for domestic mails/pink card for international) give the sender a record of who actually received the letter or package sent.

Revolving charge card: Commonly issued by major department stores and major banks, it requires a monthly payment sufficient to amortize the outstanding balance.

Scumbags: Derogatory term used to demean an individual.

Threats: An indication or warning of probable trouble.

INDEX

STOP IT!

Index

STOP IT!

Index

STOP IT!

Index

STOP IT!

Index

STOP IT!

Index

DID YOU BORROW THIS COPY?

Order additional copies of **STOP IT!** A Consumer's Guide To Effectively Stopping Collection Agency Harassment.

Please make these *idiots* at the Collection Agency *go away!* Rush _____ copies of **STOP IT!** to me. I am enclosing a **$19.95** a money order for each copy *($14.95 plus $1.16 tax and $3.84 postage/handling).*

Name: _____

Address: _____

City,
State, Zip: _____

Enclose this page (or a copy of) with your money order and mail to:

EQUITABLE MEDIA SERVICES
Post Office Box 9822-USA
Fort Worth, TX 76147-2822

or order through the **STOP IT!** "**Quick Order Line**" (toll free):
1-800-944-2236.

_____ **YES!** Please let me know when your next book, **FIX IT!** **An Insider's Look At America's Credit Bureaus** becomes available.

Equitable Media Services maintains the highest degree of privacy at all times and does not sell or disclose mailing list or client information to any outside/third party. All orders and correspondence are CONFIDENTIAL.